D1479352

The Works 2

More

Sketches from the premier Christian comedy group

Dan Rupple
and Dave Toole

MERIWETHER PUBLISHING LTD.
Colorado Springs, Colorado

Meriwether Publishing Ltd., Publisher
P.O. Box 7710
Colorado Springs, CO 80933-7710

Editor: Rhonda Wray
Typesetting: Janice Melvin and Sue Trinko
Cover design: Janice Melvin

© Copyright MM Foolish Guys
Printed in the United States of America
First Edition

Library of Congress Cataloging-in-Publication Data

Isaac Air Freight (Comedy troupe)
    Isaac Air Freight : the works 2 : more sketches from the premier Christian comedy group / [compiled by] Dan Rupple & Dave Toole.
      p.   c.m.
    ISBN 1-56608-069-X (pbk.)
    1. Christian life--Wit and humor. 2. American wit and humor.
I. Rupple, Dan, 1955-   .   II. Toole, Dave, 1953-   .   III. Title.
BV4517.I73   1997
277.3'0825'0207--dc21   96-19906
                                                          CIP

1 2 3 4 5   00   01   02   03

Contents

Publisher's Preface

Popular Christian comedy duo Isaac Air Freight pioneered the use of sketch comedy from a Christian perspective in the late seventies-early eighties through recorded albums, concert tours, radio, and television performances. When we published their first book of scripts (*Isaac Air Freight: The Works*, Meriwether Publishing Ltd., 1997), people clamored for more! Fortunately for us and for drama ministries everywhere, Isaac Air Freight (a.k.a. Dan Rupple and Dave Toole) had a whole treasure chest full of previously unpublished material in their files which became this follow-up book. When they compiled their sketches and sent them in, we were pleased and amazed to find a total of 51 gems. This book plus their first book constitutes the complete script archives of Isaac Air Freight.

To make your favorite sketches easier to locate, we have arranged them alphabetically within Part 1 and Part 2.

In Part 1, "From the Albums," many of the sketches are taken from *The Freight's Designer Album* and *Over Our Heads*. Four more of their best-selling albums, *Fun in the Son, In the Air/On the Air, Foolish Guys ... to Confound the Wise,* and *My Kingdom Come/Thy Kingdom Come* are also represented. We have tried to make these recorded sketches user-friendly for live performance through production hints and clear stage directions.

Part 2, "From the Stage," contains material from Isaac Air Freight's fourteen years of concert tours. Most of the sketches were performed live; however, some sketches didn't have the opportunity to be performed before the group disbanded.

Scripture quotations appear in some of the scripts — always paraphrased by the author(s). If you prefer, please use the Bible version of your choice. Note that the Scripture references are included for the reader/performer's reference only and should not be read aloud during performances.

A few words on performance: Use microphones as needed. Since two guys performed the majority of these sketches, obviously most of the roles were originally written for males. In many instances a female may play the part. Please feel free to substitute. Encourage your

1

audience to participate in the fun! As noted in the book, applause may always be taped, but your audience will be drawn in quickly if they help set the scene.

Performance of these scripts requires the purchase of the book. Only the buyer of the book and his/her group may use it. Please do not photocopy material for friends or acquaintances outside of your group. In order to legally photocopy any script from the book, we must have your name (or someone from your group) on record as a purchaser of the book. We ask that you respect Isaac Air Freight's generosity with their original material. They deserve to be fairly compensated for their efforts.

Although some of the sketches were written up to twenty years ago, the spiritual message of each sketch is timeless. Please feel free to update them in terms of current events, slang, and situations as you wish or, if you want to play up the seventies angle with its newfound popularity, leave as is.

Though no longer together as a performing duo, Isaac Air Freight's ministry lives on among their many fans nationwide. Whether you use this book as a memento of the group's heyday or new material for your drama ministry, we hope you will laugh and learn from the antics of the zany characters within these pages.

NOTE: The numerals running vertically down the left margin of each page of dialog are for the convenience of the director. By using them, he/she may easily direct attention to a specific passage.

Part 1
From the Albums

Are You a Fool?

By Dan Rupple

Cast: Mr. Grayson, Jake Corkscrew, Carl Corkscrew.

Setting: Mr. Grayson's office. Place a desk and chair at Center Stage, with two chairs placed together beside the desk (for the Corkscrew brothers). The intercom may be mimed. All the characters jump out a window at the end. You may use a ledge or perhaps a chair to jump from.

Props: A glass of water and pills for Mr. Grayson.

Costumes: A suit and tie for Mr. Grayson. Jake and Carl wear mechanic uniforms.

1 *(MR. GRAYSON sits behind a desk. He speaks into an intercom.)*
2 **MR. GRAYSON: Miss Tweed, send in the next client please.** *(CARL*
3 *and JAKE enter.)*
4 **CARL: Come on, Jake.**
5 **JAKE:** *(To MR. GRAYSON)* **You in charge here?**
6 **MR. GRAYSON: I'm Mr. Grayson. Welcome to Personal Evaluation.**
7 **CARL: Howdy! I'm Carl, and this here's Jake.**
8 **JAKE: We're the Corkscrew brothers.**
9 **MR. GRAYSON: Fine. Please have a seat.** *(CARL and JAKE sit.)*
10 **CARL: Thank you.**
11 **JAKE:** *(Puts hand above eyes as if looking out in the vicinity of the*
12 *"window.")* **What a view! Gosh, you've got ants down there.**
13 **MR. GRAYSON: Those are people. We're on the twelfth floor.**
14 **Now, what kind of testing are you interested in?**
15 **CARL: Well, we've got a little problem.**
16 **JAKE: Yeah, people think we're dumb.**
17 **MR. GRAYSON: Dumb?**
18 **CARL: Yeah, you know — stupid.**
19 **MR. GRAYSON: Yes, I understand. So you want to be tested to see**
20 **if you really are?**
21 **CARL: Yeah!**
22 **JAKE: Gosh, you're pretty sharp.**
23 **CARL: He's got to be, Jake; he's got his own office.**
24 **MR. GRAYSON: Look, we're running a little short on time, so let's**
25 **get started. I have a series of questions for each of you, and**
26 **this will assist us in determining the level of your intelligence,**
27 **both individually and collectively.**
28 **JAKE:** *(Laughs.)* **Collectively? Why would we need to collect**
29 **anything?**
30 **CARL: Yeah, unless we're scatterbrains or something.** *(Both laugh.*
31 *MR. GRAYSON isn't amused.)*
32 **MR. GRAYSON: Shall we begin? Question number one is for**
33 **you, Carl. If you were stranded on a deserted island, what**
34 **would you do first? A, build a hut; B, build a boat; or C, build**
35 **a fire?**

1   CARL: Well, I'd probably watch TV.
2   MR. GRAYSON: No! That's not one of the choices.
3   CARL: Could we make it one?
4   MR. GRAYSON: You don't have a television.
5   JAKE: We did before we came here, unless you know something
6   we don't know.
7   MR. GRAYSON: No, I'm saying that you don't have one on the
8   island.
9   CARL: Maybe I could borrow one from the neighbors.
10 MR. GRAYSON: There's no one else on the island!
11 CARL: Well, then I'd just take it.
12 JAKE: 'Course he'd give it back when they came home.
13 MR. GRAYSON: Let's just move on. Question number two. This is
14   for you, Jake.
15 JAKE: Gosh, thank you.
16 MR. GRAYSON: Don't mention it. Jake, I give you five cookies.
17   Now you …
18 JAKE: What kind?
19 MR. GRAYSON: Excuse me?
20 JAKE: What kind of cookies?
21 MR. GRAYSON: I don't know, this is all hypothetical. Now I give
22   you …
23 JAKE: Could I have butterscotch?
24 MR. GRAYSON: Mr. Corkscrew, it doesn't matter what kind!
25 JAKE: That's easy for you to say. I'm the one who's gotta eat 'em.
26 MR. GRAYSON: OK, Mr. Corkscrew. Now, I give you five
27   butterscotch cookies. Now if I …
28 JAKE: Could I have six?
29 MR. GRAYSON: What?
30 JAKE: I want to give one to Carl.
31 CARL: Thanks, Jake. Make mine chocolate chip.
32 MR. GRAYSON: The question says five.
33 JAKE: He's probably keeping the last one for himself.
34 MR. GRAYSON: OK! I give you six cookies. Now, if I take three
35   back, how many will you have left?

1   JAKE: Six.

2   MR. GRAYSON: No, no, I said I take three back!

3   JAKE: No you don't.

4   CARL: When it comes to cookies, Jake's pretty protective.

5   MR. GRAYSON: Let's move on to the next question.

6   JAKE: What about the cookies?

7   MR. GRAYSON: I'll get them later! Number three, Carl. If you

8   only had one more day to live, what would you do? A, write a

9   will; B, throw a party; or C, plant a tree?

10   CARL: I'd get ready to meet my Maker.

11   MR. GRAYSON: Stick to the test, Mr. Corkscrew. That is *not* one

12   of the choices.

13   JAKE: It's the only choice, if you ask me.

14   CARL: Don't you believe in God?

15   MR. GRAYSON: No, of course not.

16   CARL: You're kidding!

17   MR. GRAYSON: No. There is no such thing as God.

18   CARL: Then where'd everything come from?

19   MR. GRAYSON: You men are much too ignorant to understand

20   these complex matters.

21   JAKE: Try us.

22   MR. GRAYSON: Well, there was a big bang.

23   CARL: A big what?

24   MR. GRAYSON: Bang, an explosion!

25   CARL: And it all just happened?

26   MR. GRAYSON: Yes.

27   JAKE: Mountains, rivers, condos — you mean everything?

28   MR. GRAYSON: Yes, it's a scientific fact. *(CARL and JAKE laugh.)*

29   I told you you wouldn't understand it.

30   CARL: Now, wait a minute. We get it.

31   JAKE: Sure. I heard about it on TV. There was a big bang, and

32   then a bunch of squiggly things turned into fish, and then the

33   fish walked out of the lake and grew hair, then one day they

34   shaved off the hair and they became truck drivers.

35   CARL: Is that about it?

1 MR. GRAYSON: Pretty much. *(Pause. CARL and JAKE laugh*
2   *hysterically.)*
3 CARL: I hope there isn't another bang. We may turn into office
4   furniture.
5 MR. GRAYSON: Look, let's just finish the test. Jake, this last
6   question is for you. You are standing in front of a table. On the
7   table is a candle and a book of matches. Suddenly the lights go
8   off and someone yells, "This is a power failure!" What would
9   you do?
10 JAKE: I'd check to see if the guy who yelled had our television.
11 MR. GRAYSON: Mr. Corkscrew, he doesn't have your television.
12 JAKE: Then what's he doing on a deserted island?
13 CARL: Sounds pretty suspicious, if you ask me.
14 MR. GRAYSON: No, no one stole your TV set!
15 JAKE: Then how come Carl couldn't watch it on the island? Wait
16   a minute. I get it. That was a trick question, wasn't it?
17 MR. GRAYSON: What?
18 JAKE: How could there be a power failure on a deserted island?
19 MR. GRAYSON: Why me? In all my years I've seen all kinds, but
20   never anyone as stupid as this. You're imbeciles!
21 JAKEand CARL: *(Together)* We are?!
22 MR. GRAYSON: You're complete idiots!
23 CARL: Gosh, you got our test scores back already?
24 JAKE: I guess we came from dumb monkeys. *(CARL and JAKE*
25   *laugh.)*
26 MR. GRAYSON: Out! Get out! You're driving me crazy. I never
27   want to see you again!
28 CARL: Come on, Jake. I think something upset him.
29 JAKE: Nice meeting you. *(CARL and JAKE exit. MR. GRAYSON*
30   *takes pills. CARL and JAKE return.)* Wait a minute — what
31   about my cookies?
32 MR. GRAYSON: That's it! I'm jumping. *(MR. GRAYSON jumps out*
33   *of "window.")*
34 JAKE: Gosh.
35 CARL: I bet he believes in God now.

1   **JAKE: Wait a minute. He's got our cookies.**
2   **CARL: Come on, Jake!** *(CARL and JAKE jump.)*
3
4
5
6
7
8
9
10
11
12
13
14
15
16
17
18
19
20
21
22
23
24
25
26
27
28
29
30
31
32
33
34
35

Back for the Future — Moses McFly

By Dan Rupple

Cast: Doc, Marty, Moses McFly, Biff Pharaoh, God

Setting: The parking lot of a mall in the middle of the night. Two chairs at Stage Right represent a car.

Props: A skateboard, tennis racket and ball, grotesque mask and two guitars.

Costumes: Doc wears a lab coat and has wild hair. Marty wears jeans, a down-filled vest and a flannel shirt. Moses McFly wears a biblical robe with a pocket protector on it, sandals and a long white beard. Biff Pharaoh wears tennis gear.

Sound Effects: Car racing, zoom, Egyptian music, crash. *Suggested music:* "The Power of Love" Intro *(Written by Johnny Colla, Chris Hayes and Huey Lewis, and recorded on* The Best of Huey Lewis and the News *[1996], Elektra #61977-2).*

1   *(DOC enters. He is worried.)*
2   DOC: I can't believe it! This is horrible. This could change the
3   history of mankind. The history of eternity! *(Enter MARTY on*
4   *his skateboard.)*
5   MARTY: Doc! Doc, what's the big deal? I was sound asleep.
6   DOC: Marty, we've got an emergency. There's a problem in the
7   past.
8   MARTY: Big deal. This is the nineties. Who cares about the past?
9   DOC: But Marty, if you don't resolve the past, there'll be no future.
10   MARTY: If you're talking about Iraq, it's OK. We won.
11   DOC: No. Way back, Marty, to the days of Pharaoh in Egypt. Your
12   great-to-the-ninety-seventh-power grandfather doesn't want
13   to believe in God.
14   MARTY: Well, that's his problem.
15   DOC: But he's got to, Marty. He's got to stand up to Pharaoh.
16   MARTY: My great-to-the-ninety-seventh-power grandfather?
17   DOC: That's right, Marty, Moses McFly!
18   MARTY: I'm related to Moses? No wonder I never liked ham. But
19   what can I do about it?
20   DOC: I've invented a time machine. It's right here in this
21   DeLorean.
22   MARTY: This is a DeLorean? No wonder these things didn't sell.
23   I've seen folding chairs that looked better.
24   DOC: You get inside, and I'll send you back.
25   MARTY: No way, Doc. I'm not a good traveler. I get sick just
26   riding the school bus. Why don't you go?
27   DOC: I can't. *Taxi*'s on tonight. It's my favorite show. I never miss
28   it. You've got to, Marty. If Moses doesn't free Israel, we're
29   finished. No nation. No savior. No future … and worst of all,
30   no sketch! Maybe that's not so bad.
31   MARTY: OK, Doc, I'll do it.
32   DOC: Good boy, Marty. *(MARTY hops in the car.)*
33   MARTY: How do you work this?
34   DOC: I'll set the dial. *(DOC pantomimes setting the dial.)* Now you
35   just get it up to eighty-eight miles per hour. And Marty, God

1   be with you! *(DOC exits.)*

2   MARTY: He'd better be. If I get another speeding ticket, I'll lose

3   my license. Hey, it's not funny. Why do you think I have to

4   ride a skateboard through this entire movie? OK, here goes.

5   *(The sounds of a car racing, a zoom and Egyptian music are*

6   *heard.)* Wow, I made it. Ancient Egypt. Wow, look at that guy

7   with the arthritic arms ... walk like an Egyptian. *(Enter*

8   *MOSES McFLY. He is talking to himself.)*

9   MOSES: I can't do it. Pharaoh's a big guy. I can't just walk up to

10   him and say, "Let my people go." He'll kill me.

11   MARTY: Boy, he doesn't look anything like Charlton Heston.

12   Excuse me, are you Moses McFly?

13   MOSES: That's me. Do I know you?

14   MARTY: No, my name's Marty.

15   MOSES: Hi, Marty.

16   MARTY: But I know you. You're famous.

17   MOSES: Oh, gee. I never wanted to be famous. I just wanted to

18   quietly run my pizza shop.

19   MARTY: Pizza shop?

20   MOSES: Yeah, but then the calls started — hundreds a day. But I

21   kept telling them, I don't deliver!

22   MARTY: But Moses, you've got to deliver. That's your calling.

23   MOSES: But Marty, I can't face Pharaoh. He's a lot bigger than I

24   am.

25   MARTY: Pharaoh? He's a buzzhead. Look, God's not asking you

26   to wrestle with him. All you've got to do is talk with him.

27   MOSES: Oh, I'm not too good at confrontation. I get flustered at

28   the beep of an answering machine ... and they haven't even

29   invented them yet.

30   MARTY: Sure you're scared, but you're on a mission from God!

31   Trust me on this one.

32   MOSES: Oh, I don't know, Marty.

33   MARTY: Look, I gotta get back ...

34   MOSES: I know, *Family Ties* and all.

35   MARTY: Hey, you don't like that show? It's the secret of my

1   success. You know, Moses, if you obey God on this one,
2   someday he'll give you more commandments — probably ten
3   of them. *(MARTY exits.)*
4   MOSES: Huh. With my luck, I'll probably drop them.
5   GOD: *(Off-stage)* Moses.
6   MOSES: Oh no, God's speaking to me again. You're not going to
7   scorch my shrubs again, are ya? Last time my wife had me
8   doing yard work for a week.
9   GOD: Moses, do not fear Pharaoh. I will back up your demands
10   with plagues upon Egypt until my people are free.
11   MOSES: Plagues? What kinds of plagues?
12   GOD: Well, lots of things.
13   MOSES: For instance?
14   GOD: Bugs, blood, boils ... and worst of all ...
15   MOSES: Milli Vanilli?
16   GOD: No, death.
17   MOSES: Uh, that could hurt.
18   GOD: Go forth, Moses. You will be Israel's deliverer.
19   MOSES: There it is again. I don't deliver! *(Enter BIFF PHARAOH*
20   *holding a tennis racket and ball.)* Oh, hello, Pharaoh Sir.
21   BIFF: McFly! Hello, anybody home? *(Knocks on MOSES' head.)*
22   How many time have I told you? Call me Biff.
23   MOSES: OK, Biff.
24   BIFF: OK, now get over to the other side of the net and hit the ball.
25   MOSES: No, Biff, I can't do that.
26   BIFF: McFly? Are you telling me that Moses won't serve in
27   Pharaoh's court?
28   MOSES: No, it's just that there's something I gotta say.
29   BIFF: What, McFly? You got something on your chest? *(BIFF*
30   *points to MOSES' shirt. MOSES looks down, then BIFF flips his*
31   *finger up.)* Don't be so gullible, McFly. Now if you've got
32   something to say, spit it out.
33   MOSES: OK, Biff. Let my people go.
34   BIFF: And if I don't, what are you gonna do about it?
35   MOSES: This! *(MOSES does a double whammy, but nothing*

1   *happens.)*

2   **BIFF: What's that? The Watusi? Look, I don't have all day.**

3   **Maybe I can find that McEnroe kid.** *(BIFF exits.)*

4   **MOSES: Way to go, God. I do my part, and what happens? I'm a**

5   **big Moses McFlop with Egg McMuffin all over my face.** *(A*

6   *supernatural crash is heard. BIFF enters wearing a grotesque*

7   *mask.)*

8   **BIFF: What'd ya do to me, McFly? My face looks like one of your**

9   **pizzas.**

10   **MOSES: That's just the start, Biff. Now let my people go.**

11   **BIFF: OK, OK. Just make it stop.**

12   **MOSES: We'll see. Now get!**

13   **BIFF: OK, anything you say, Mr. McFly.** *(A wimpy BIFF exits.)*

14   **MOSES:** *(Looks up.)* **Well, God, we did it. We stood up to Pharaoh.**

15   **No more bullying around Moses McFly. Now the Israelites**

16   **are free from old buzzhead, and all from obeying God. Well,**

17   **we pretty well ripped the whole move now ... except for one**

18   **thing ...**

19   **MARTY:** *(Off-stage)* **Rock 'n' roll!**

20   **MOSES: Hit it, Marty!** *(MARTY enters with guitars. MOSES and*

21   *MARTY sing "Moses Do Good" to the tune of "Johnny Be*

22   *Good.")*

23

24   ***SONG:*** "Moses Do Good" (Lyrics by Dan Rupple and Dave Toole)

25

26   **MOSES and MARTY:** *(Singing)* **Way down in olden Egypt, down**

27   **Pharaoh's way,**

28   **There was a band of people makin' bricks all day.**

29   **Workin' and a-slavin' in the hot desert sun,**

30   **While Pharaoh and his buddies sat around havin' fun.**

31   **Jehovah made a vow to give them liberty,**

32   **But he needed a man to set his people free.**

33

34   *Chorus:*

35   **Go, go, let my people go,**

1	Go, go, let my people go,
2	Go, go, let my people go,
3	Go, go, let my people go,
4	Go, go, Moses do good.
5	
6	Well, God told Moses, "Mo, you're my main man,
7	And you will be the leader of the Jewish band."
8	His people gonna walk those miles around
9	And follow that cloud until the sun goes down.
10	There's gonna come a day they'll reach the Promised Land
11	If they put their trust upon the great "I Am."
12	
13	Repeat Chorus
14	
15	Guitar solo *(MOSES and MARTY may dance around the stage*
16	a la *Chuck Berry.)*
17	
18	Repeat Chorus
19	
20	
21	
22	
23	
24	
25	
26	
27	
28	
29	
30	
31	
32	
33	
34	
35	

Crazy Christians

By Dan Rupple

Cast: Announcers 1 and 2, Sheriff, Christian, Buck Wheezer.

Setting: The set of a television commercial.

Props: None.

Costumes: A uniform for the Sheriff. Christian and Buck may be dressed casually.

1   *(Optional music cue)*
2   **ANNOUNCER 1:** *(From Off-stage)* **Watch out, world. Something**
3   **big is coming your way.** They're alive, they're bold, they're
4   **friendly, they're the Crazy Christians!** Walkin' down your
5   **street, sharing with your neighbors, sharing with your**
6   **children, and yes, even sharing with you!** *(Optional music cue)*
7   **Last Supper Pictures presents** *The Crazy Christians.* **There's**
8   **nothing else like it. They carry a Bible in their hand and wear**
9   **a smile on their face. They touch people's lives wherever they**
10   **go. Many may laugh in mockery, but soon you'll be laughing**
11   **with joy as you meet up with the Crazy Christians! You'll see**
12   **scenes like this ...** *(SHERIFF enters.)*
13   **SHERIFF:** Yeah, I'm the sheriff in this town. Since them Crazy
14   Christians came through, my jail is empty. I haven't had a
15   thing to do for weeks now. 'Course Clem, he's the fella that
16   owns the liquor store, he's gonna teach me how to crochet
17   later this afternoon, but since those Crazy Christians came
18   through here, things just ain't been the same ... *(SHERIFF*
19   *exits. Optional music cue)*
20   **ANNOUNCER 1:** Yes, where Crazy Christians go, joy and love
21   follow. Watch out! They're everywhere, spreading the Good
22   News ... *(CHRISTIAN and BUCK enter from opposite sides.)*
23   **CHRISTIAN:** Hi!
24   **BUCK:** How you doing?
25   **CHRISTIAN:** Great! Did you know that Jesus died on the cross for
26   you?
27   **BUCK:** You're kidding.
28   **CHRISTIAN:** Nope.
29   **BUCK:** For me, Buck Wheezer? *(CHRISTIAN and BUCK pantomime*
30   *a conversation.)*
31   **ANNOUNCER 1:** Yes, soon even you will be saying things like,
32   "Praise the Lord," "In Jesus' Name," and "It's all gonna
33   burn." No more will you be filled with fear, frustration and
34   depression, when your life is touched by those Crazy
35   Christians! The world is ready. Christ is returning. See it! And

18

1   believe it! *Crazy Christians* is appearing everywhere.
2   **ANNOUNCER 2:** *(Also Off-stage)* **Rated B. Only those believing**
3   **will be admitted.**
4
5
6
7
8
9
10
11
12
13
14
15
16
17
18
19
20
21
22
23
24
25
26
27
28
29
30
31
32
33
34
35

Cult

By Dave Toole

Cast: Announcer, Son, Dad, Mom (non-speaking).

Setting: The television set of a commercial. Place a card table and chairs at Center Stage.

Props: A board game with a spinner and two slips of paper.

Costumes: Casual clothing for all.

1   (MOM, DAD and SON sit at a card table, playing a board game
2   throughout the sketch.)
3   ANNOUNCER: (From Off-stage) **What are these people doing?**
4   **They're playing the home version of a game millions of people**
5   **are playing worldwide, *Cult*—the most realistic family**
6   **pastime since electronic football! It's fun, and so easy!**
7   **First, you'll need new Scriptures, but what will you do?**
8   **Declare your own personal proclamations holy? Make up**
9   **whole new volumes of "inspired Scripture"? Or just rewrite**
10   **the Bible to suit your own beliefs?**
11   **Next, it's on to big business. How much should your**
12   **followers pay to belong to your church? Spin the "Money**
13   **Dial" and see …**
14 SON: **OK! Neato!** (Reading his slip of paper) **"Your followers must**
15   **sacrifice all their present holdings and future income to you."**
16   **Oh boy!**
17 ANNOUNCER: **Soon you'll be out there knocking on doors and**
18   **selling flowers in airports, making millions in spiritual**
19   **deception. 'Round and 'round the board you go, building up**
20   **members and money — but watch out!**
21 DAD: (Reading his slip of paper) **Oh, no. "You and your followers**
22   **commit mass suicide. Place all your holdings in the**
23   **Communal Chest." Ohhhh!**
24 ANNOUNCER: **Yes, it's the Grim Reaper card. But that's only one**
25   **of the hazards. Taxes, public relations, internal politics and**
26   **many more.**
27   **How do you win? Ah, that's the catch: You don't. Just like**
28   **real life, everyone who gets involved with the cults loses. No**
29   **matter how much you put in or how much you get out, you'll**
30   **be eternally shortchanged.**
31   ***Cult*. The game for people who want to play with fire but**
32   **don't want to get burned.**
33
34
35

E. F. Bullish

By Dave Toole

Cast: Announcer, Porter Boswell, Stevens, Sims (non-speaking role).

Setting: A busy restaurant. Place a card table with tablecloth and chairs at Center Stage, with dishes on the table as desired.

Props: None.

Costumes: Suits and ties.

Sound Effects: You may have a background tape of "restaurant noise" (music, chatter, clanging dishes).

1　*(PORTER, SIMS and STEVENS sit at the table.)*
2　PORTER: Now listen, Stevens, the reason I called this little
3　　meeting was to see how you feel about the Amalgamated
4　　Corporations deal. Now, we've checked with our broker, and
5　　he feels that it's a great deal for both your company and ours,
6　　so what do you say?
7　STEVENS: Ah, Mr. Boswell, I'm still not sure what to say. Who's
8　　your broker?
9　PORTER: Ha! Who's my broker? Ha-ha! Did you hear that, Sims?
10　　He wants to know who our broker is! *(Laughter)* My boy, our
11　　broker is E.F. Bullish ... *(Silence as tape is stopped. Pause)* and
12　　when E.F. Bullish talks, people listen!
13　STEVENS: Well, Mr. Boswell, we do things a little differently at
14　　our board meetings. You see, after I read all the reports and
15　　discuss the possibilities, I pray about what I should do. I
16　　literally ask God to show me. After all, the Bible does say, "If
17　　anyone lacks wisdom, let him ask" (James 1:5, author's
18　　paraphrase). So I guess you could say my broker is Jesus
19　　Christ, and Jesus Christ says ...*(Pause. Restaurant noise*
20　　*continues.)*
21　PORTER: Yes, yes?
22　STEVENS: Wait a second. I said, my broker is Jesus Christ, and
23　　Jesus says ...
24　ANNOUNCER: *(From Off-stage)* Isn't it a shame? Everywhere you
25　　go, people are searching for the answer to their problems, and
26　　yet, when Jesus talks — no one listens.
27
28
29
30
31
32
33
34
35

Ed Herman's Talk Radio — Ed Cares

By Dan Rupple

Cast: Ed Herman, Caller #1 (female), Caller #2 (male), Caller #3 (female), Caller #4, Caller #5.

Setting: A talk radio studio. Place a table and chair at Center Stage.

Props: Headphones and a push-button telephone.

Costumes: Casual attire.

Sound Effects: Gunshot, optional theme music.

Notes: The callers are Off-stage, speaking into a microphone.

1   ED: OK, it's about a quarter past the hour on Ed Herman's talk
2   radio show. Give me a call. You got a problem, you need an
3   ear, call me, Ed Herman. I care. It's a cold, complex world out
4   there, and maybe you need a little understanding. That's why
5   I'm here. I care about you. Just dial ED CARES. Line one is
6   flashing. Hello, you're on the Ed Herman show.
7   CALLER #1: Ed, I'm a widow with three small children, and I've
8   been evicted. What should I do?
9   ED: Do whatever you want to do. Look, you've got a brain, don't
10   you?
11   CALLER #1: Yeah, I just thought that …
12   ED: You just thought … Come on, lady, give me a break. *(Hangs up.)*
13   Evicted. She probably doesn't even have a place to stay. Big
14   deal. I'm Ed Herman. I care about you. Let's go to line two.
15   CALLER #2: Yeah, Ed?
16   ED: You got it.
17   CALLER #2: Oh, Ed. Man, I need help, man. You got to help me,
18   Ed. I think I OD'd.
19   ED: Calm down. I'll talk you back to reality, pal. What's your
20   name?
21   CALLER #2: Murray.
22   ED: OK, Murray. Now what did you take?
23   CALLER #2: Oh, you name it, Ed. I got drugs all over the
24   apartment. I'm flying, Ed.
25   ED: Great. Well, look out for small aircraft.
26   CALLER #2: What?
27   ED: There's some small aircraft reported in your area.
28   CALLER #2: Oh, man, what a bummer! *(ED hangs up.)*
29   ED: Blowing people's minds on Ed Herman's talk radio show.
30   Before we go to line three, I want to talk about tomorrow's
31   show. Tomorrow we have a special topic. Our topic is illegal
32   aliens, and our guest will be an officer from the Federal
33   Immigration Board. So if you know any illegal aliens, or
34   maybe you're one yourself, be sure to call in, give your name
35   and address, and we'll be sure to help you out. Just another

1   service of Ed Herman's show, because I care about you. Let's
2   go to line three. Hello, you're on with Ed Herman.
3   CALLER #3: Ed, I want a divorce!
4   ED: Mavis, why are you calling me on the air?
5   CALLER #3: It's the only place I could reach you.
6   ED: Mavis ...
7   CALLER #3: Face it, Ed. Our marriage is a wash. I'm taking the
8   kids with me.
9   ED: Kids? I didn't know we had kids.
10 CALLER #3: What did you think they were? House plants?
11 ED: Mavis, look, I can't talk now. I'm helping people with their
12 problems.
13 CALLER #3: You're gonna regret the day you married me! *(ED*
14 *hangs up.)*
15 ED: Women callers! What a pain. Are there any men out there?
16 Give me a call. Let's go to line four. With any luck it'll be a
17 man.
18 CALLER #4: Hello? Is this Ed Herman?
19 ED: *¡Hola! ¿Que pasa?*
20 CALLER #4: Is this Ed Herman? *(ED speaks Spanish gibberish.)*
21 Oh, I'm sorry, I must have the wrong number. *(Gunshot*
22 *sounds. ED hangs up.)*
23 ED: No sense of humor, I tell you. Let's wrap it up. Line five, you're
24 on with Ed Herman.
25 CALLER #5: Yeah, Ed, I'm a first-time caller. I've been listening
26 to your show, and frankly, I can't believe you.
27 ED: What do you mean?
28 CALLER #5: I mean, you haven't helped anybody. Don't you have
29 any sense of caring or compassion?
30 ED: Of course I do ...
31 CALLER #5: How do you sleep at night?
32 ED: Horizontal. How do you sleep?
33 CALLER #5: Very funny, Ed. Come on Ed, you don't care about
34 anyone. All I've heard is Ed cares, Ed cares, but you couldn't
35 care less.

1   **ED:** Oh, yeah? Well, who have you helped today?

2   **CALLER #5:** You're a rip-off, Herman. You don't even ... *(ED*

3   *hangs up.)*

4   **ED:** Says I don't care. What a joke. I've got to care, I'm on the

5   radio. Oh well, that's about it for now. Thanks for listening.

6   Join me tomorrow for Ed Herman's talk radio show. You got

7   a problem, give me a call. If you're down and lonely, turn to

8   this man, Ed Herman. I care abut you. So until next time,

9   remember — Ed cares. He really does. *(Optional theme music)*

10

11

12

13

14

15

16

17

18

19

20

21

22

23

24

25

26

27

28

29

30

31

32

33

34

35

Fadscene — Punk vs. Preppie

By Dan Rupple

Cast: Theda Williams, Rash Melton, Charlene "Leenie" Menderthal.

Setting: The *Fadscene* television set. There are three chairs at Center Stage — Theda's in the middle, Rash is to her right, and Leenie is to her left. The guests' chairs may be angled in slightly.

Props: None.

Costumes: Theda should wear a suit. Rash should wear rock star attire (torn jeans, black leather, wild hair, etc.). Leenie should wear an Izod brand polo shirt, khaki pants and penny loafers.

Sound Effects: Optional theme music.

1   (*THEDA sits at Center Stage. LEENIE sits at THEDA's right and*
2   *RASH sits at her left. Optional theme music plays.*)
3   ANNOUNCER: (*Off-stage*) **Fadscene, with your host and moderator,**
4   **Theda Williams.**
5   THEDA: **I'm Theda Williams. Tonight on** *Fadscene,* **I'll be examining**
6   **two current fads as we debate punk versus preppie. With me**
7   **is preppie advocate, Charlene "Leenie" Menderthal.**
8   LEENIE: **I mean, my total life was being threatened. I got a B- in**
9   **Poli Sci. If Mummy hadn't talked with Teach, I would've**
10   **barfed right on my alligator.**
11   THEDA: **And I'll be talking with punk leader Rash Melton.**
12   RASH: **I think my jewelry has purpose. Who's to say when you're**
13   **gonna need a safety pin?**
14   THEDA: **Enjoy the fireworks as we investigate two fads that**
15   **dictate our lifestyles. Will they become cultural dinosaurs like**
16   **the disco craze and the hippie movement before it?**
17   LEENIE: **Ewww. The dork who cut your hair seems to have cut**
18   **your clothes, too.**
19   RASH: **My clothes are a statement of the violence that has**
20   **shattered our lives on the street.**
21   LEENIE: **I think you mean in the gutter.**
22   RASH: **I'm gonna pin my designer label right on your designer**
23   **head.**
24   THEDA: (*Stands.*) **That's** *Fadscene,* **tonight at nine. Regardless of**
25   **what you base your life on, before it's out of style, join me,**
26   **Theda Williams, for** *Fadscene.* **I'll talk about anything, as**
27   **long as it's as trendy as this show.** (*Optional theme music plays.*)
28   ANNOUNCER: *Fadscene,* **right here on this station — for now.**
29
30
31
32
33
34
35

Generic Phone Company

By Dan Rupple

Cast: Announcer, Man, Woman.

Setting: Television commercial set. Place two chairs at Center Stage.

Props: Two telephones.

Costumes: Casual clothing. Man may wear black and white, in keeping with the generic theme.

Sound Effects: Ringing telephone.

Notes: This particular piece was written in 1983, before "976" numbers and during the initial influx of generic products in stores. Although it isn't essential, background music while the announcer speaks adds to the commercial feel.

1   *(MAN and WOMAN with telephones sit at Center Stage and*
2   *freeze until it is time for them to speak.)*
3   ANNOUNCER: *(From Off-stage)* **You've probably noticed at your**
4   **local supermarket, how many products have the word**
5   **"generic" on them ... generic eggs, generic milk, even generic**
6   **tissue. You don't know where they came from, and you don't**
7   **care. Why? Because they're cheaper. They're cheaper because**
8   **you're not paying extra for the name.** *(MAN picks up phone*
9   *and begins to dial.)* **But what about the phone company? Isn't**
10   **it about time to have generic phone calls? You bet it is!** *(Phone*
11   *rings. WOMAN picks up phone.)*
12   MAN: **Hello?**
13   WOMAN: *(Puzzled)* **Hello?**
14   MAN: **Hi! You don't know me, but I'm calling from Kankakee,**
15   **Illinois, and this is costing me practically nothing ...** *(MAN*
16   *and WOMAN pantomime conversation as ANNOUNCER speaks.)*
17   ANNOUNCER: **Have you ever just wanted to talk with someone?**
18   **Well, why call someone you know? It'll cost a fortune. And**
19   **why? Because you know who they are. You're paying for the**
20   **name. Call a complete stranger and save!** *(Phone conversation*
21   *audibly resumes.)*
22   MAN: **So, how's the weather in Phoenix?**
23   WOMAN: *(Getting disgusted)* **It's hot ... who is this?**
24   MAN: **Nah, this is a generic phone call. If I tell you who I am, the**
25   **rate goes up. So, did you see the news last night?**
26   WOMAN: **How did you get my number?** *(MAN and WOMAN*
27   *pantomime conversation as ANNOUNCER speaks.)*
28   ANNOUNCER: **The generic phone company. When you want to**
29   **talk and anyone will do. The generic phone company. Reach**
30   **out and touch someone — anyone.** *(Phone conversation*
31   *continues audibly.)*
32   MAN: **So ... you ever get to Illinois?**
33   WOMAN: **Well, no, but isn't it somewhere near Chicago?**
34   *(Background music fades out.)*
35

KBAM, Your Nuclear Fallout Station

By Dan Rupple

Cast: Disc Jockey.

Setting: None. (Audio-only sketch.)

Props: None.

Costumes: None.

1   *(Suggested music intro, "The Beat Goes On" by Sonny and Cher*
2   *[Best of Sonny and Cher, Rhino Records, 1991], plays, then fades*
3   *out.)*
4   DISC JOCKEY: You're listening to **KBAM**, your nuclear fallout
5   station for the greater Northwest sector. KBAM weather
6   forecast for day three after the big blast: hot, highs in the
7   nineties, and scattered mushroom clouds. Chances are ninety-
8   five percent for a heavy acid rain sometime this evening.
9   KBAM sports for and update on that Raiders-Packers game.
10   The Raiders were annihilated. Not by the Packers; they were
11   just annihilated. We'll be going to our phones in a little bit,
12   and we've cooked up something really special. You know in
13   the past three days, we've each lost many loved ones, but I
14   know that deep down inside, we're all wondering how this all
15   affects Victoria Principal. Well, I'll be talking to Victoria
16   "The Body" Principal on the phone from her shelter, so stay
17   tuned. Say, Mom, if your kids are getting a little fed up with
18   canned rations, Sal's Market has fresh cucumbers at the low
19   price of nine cents a ton. Yes, lately Sal's been growing them
20   big, and you'll just light up when you bite into one of Sal's
21   fresh cucumbers. So bring your truck by now and pick one
22   up. You're listening to KBAM, your nuclear fallout station.
23   Kick back, don't worry about a thing and enjoy the fireworks.
24   And now let's listen to that great hit from the fifties, "Sha
25   Boom, Sha Boom." *(Suggested song, "Sha Boom, Sha Boom" by*
26   *The Crew Cuts [Mercury, 1953], plays, then fades out.)*
27
28
29
30
31
32
33
34
35

KUSS

By Dave Toole

Cast: Announcer, KUSS (two or more rockers).

Setting: Rock concert.

Props: Electric guitars and amplifiers.

Costumes: Faces painted with black and white makeup in patterns, wild long hair, black leather rock star attire.

Notes: The rock band doesn't have any lines — they just jump around, act outrageous and make screeching noises with their electric guitars. Just make sure the Announcer can be heard over the noise!

1   ANNOUNCER: *(From Off-stage)* **If you've got a heart of stone and**
2   **you're ready to sell your soul to rock and roll, why waste your**
3   **time with Devoid or Blandie? You're ready for KUSS.** *(KUSS*
4   *members run in, playing their guitars.)* **They're more revolting**
5   **than drag, more disgusting than punk. With a sound that feels**
6   **like acid in your ears!** *(Screeching and wailing guitars)* **Go out**
7   **and seize a copy of their debut album,** *Teenage Reprobate,*
8   **featuring their hot new single, "Malted Slugs."** *(KUSS*
9   *members jump and flail around.)* **KUSS. You can call it art, you**
10 **can call it rock, you can even call it music. But one thing's for**
11 **certain: They don't have a message — just a mission, to drag**
12 **you down to the depths of hell itself and keep you there. Get**
13 **down as far as you can go with KUSS. They aren't bad,**
14 **they're wretched. KUSS, on Quagmire records and tapes.**
15 *(KUSS plays more distorted "music" to close.)*
16
17
18
19
20
21
22
23
24
25
26
27
28
29
30
31
32
33
34
35

Lance and Norman at the Drive-in

By Dan Rupple and Dave Toole

Cast: Lance, Norman.

Setting: A drive-in movie theater. Stage Right is the bathroom area. Stage Left is Norman's car, which may be as simple as two chairs placed together.

Props: Flask (the "booze").

Costumes: Lance wears very casual teenage clothing. Norman dresses like a nerd.

Sound Effect: Toilet flushing.

1   *(LANCE runs in from Stage Left to bathroom area at Stage Right.*
2   *He is panicked and looks totally disheveled.)*
3   **LANCE:** *(To audience)* **I can't believe it. I must be the most**
4   **unlucky guy in the whole world. It's Friday night here at the**
5   **drive-in. I'm with some of the guys, and we were all standing**
6   **around Duke Meisner's new car. He's the captain of the**
7   **football team. He's like a mountain with arms. We were all**
8   **drinking some wine, and I don't know why, but all of a**
9   **sudden, I threw up all over the hood. And Duke gets out of the**
10   **car and says, "I'm going to kill you!" He started chasing me**
11   **around. He's gonna kill me. I might as well have puked on**
12   **Arnold Schwartzenegger. My life is in the dumpster.** *(Toilet*
13   *flushes. LANCE panics.)* **It's him. It's him. It's The Terminator!**
14   *(LANCE falls on the ground, groveling. NORMAN, the nerd,*
15   *enters from Stage Right.)* **Please, mercy, Duke. Don't kill me.**
16   **Don't rip my arms off and beat my head with them. Please,**
17   **I'm begging you.**
18   **NORMAN: Hi, Lance.**
19   **LANCE: Norman? What are you doing?**
20   **NORMAN: Well, chess club got out a little early, and I thought I'd**
21   **catch a flick. Gee, Lance, you don't look too good. You're all**
22   **green and stuff. What, the movie kinda scaring you?**
23   **LANCE: Are you kidding? I've seen this movie eight times. You're**
24   **forgetting, this is my stomping ground.**
25   **NORMAN: What, the bathroom?**
26   **LANCE: Not the bathroom. The drive-in! You know what it says**
27   **under my picture in the yearbook, don't you?**
28   **NORMAN: Turn the page?**
29   **LANCE: No, above that. "Live to park, park to live."** *(LANCE pulls*
30   *a flask out of his pocket and takes a swig.)*
31   **NORMAN: Lance, is that alcohol?**
32   **LANCE: Yeah. How about a cocktail, shrimp?**
33   **NORMAN: No thanks, Lance. I don't drink. I get dizzy just**
34   **cleaning my tape deck.**
35   **LANCE: Look, Norman, as your best friend, it's my duty to**

1   introduce you to the finer things in life. Take a whiff.
2   *(NORMAN smells it, then lets out a huge sneeze.)* **Come on,**
3   **Norman, you got to be careful. This is one of the finest**
4   **imported wines in the world. Boone's Farm Strawberry Swill.**
5   NORMAN: **No thanks, Lance. Alcohol clashes with my allergy**
6   **medicine. I'd better get back to my car.**
7   LANCE: **Hey, Norman, before you do, do me a favor.**
8   NORMAN: **Sure, Lance, what is it?**
9   LANCE: **Could you see if Duke Meisner is out there?**
10   NORMAN: **Duke Meisner?**
11   LANCE: **Yeah.**
12   NORMAN: **OK, sure.** *(Looks Off-stage Left.)* **Oh yeah, there he is.**
13   **Hey Duke, over here!**
14   LANCE: **No, Norman! What are you doing? I can't see Duke right**
15   **now!**
16   NORMAN: **What — do you owe him money or something?**
17   LANCE: **Look, Norman, I don't have time to lie to you right now.**
18   **I threw up all over Duke's new car.**
19   NORMAN: **You threw up on Duke Meisner's new car?**
20   LANCE: **Yes.**
21   NORMAN: **You're dead meat, Lance. He's gonna kill you.**
22   LANCE: *(Looks Off-stage Left.)* **Oh no, he's coming over here.**
23   **Look, I can't talk to him ... but** *you* **can talk to him.**
24   NORMAN: **Me?**
25   LANCE: **Yeah.** *You* **called him over here. I'm gonna hide in the**
26   **bathroom stall. Get rid of him, Norman!** *(LANCE exits, to hide*
27   *in the bathroom "stall" at Off-stage Right.)*
28   NORMAN: *(Speaks Off-stage Left to imaginary Duke.)* **Oh hi, Duke.**
29   **Uh, me? Oh, I just wanted to tell you how much I enjoyed**
30   **your football game last week. Are those five guys still in**
31   **the hospital? Oh? So when are their funerals? Uh, Lance**
32   **Stocker? No, I haven't seen him. You know, I think he went**
33   **home early. There's a Wayne Newton special on tonight. He**
34   **likes to catch those things. Uh-huh, sure, if I see him, I'll tell**
35   **him you said hello. See ya later, big fella.** *(To LANCE at Off-*

1   *stage Right)* **OK … coast is clear.** *(LANCE enters.)*
2   **LANCE: Wayne Newton? I can't believe it! What'd you go and tell**
3   **him that for?**
4   **NORMAN: Well, it's all I could think of.**
5   **LANCE: Norman, I've got a reputation. What are you trying to do,**
6   **kill me?**
7   **NORMAN: Well, I'm president of his fan club. I thought I'd help**
8   **Wayne out a little.**
9   **LANCE: Well, come on, let's get to your car before you mess**
10   **something else up.**
11   **NORMAN: That's a good idea. It's safe there.** *(The guys cross to*
12   *NORMAN's car at Stage Left. NORMAN gets in the driver's seat.*
13   *LANCE sits in the front passenger seat.)* **Lance, you'll have to**
14   **get in the back seat when my date gets back.**
15   **LANCE: Your what?**
16   **NORMAN: My date. See, it's the craziest thing. I'm sitting at Bible**
17   **study the other day, and I saw this girl, so I say, "Hey girl,**
18   **would you like …"**
19   **LANCE: Hey, that's not a bad idea. Norman, this is brilliant.**
20   **You're here on your first date. I'm king of the drive-in. I'll get**
21   **in the back seat. Then when your date gets back, I can hide in**
22   **the back seat and give you some pointers.**
23   **NORMAN: Pointers?**
24   **LANCE: Yeah. Tips on how to score.**
25   **NORMAN: Oh, no, Lance, I'm not trying to score. I'm not even**
26   **playing the game. What you're talking about, it's just not my**
27   **style.**
28   **LANCE: That's a good place to start. Style. Norman, look at**
29   **yourself. You just don't have any style. Now take me, for**
30   **instance. I'm a carefully crafted mixture of Don Johnson,**
31   **Indiana Jones and Bruce Springsteen. This is not the Lance**
32   **Stocker my parents gave birth to.**
33   **NORMAN: Boy, are your parents gonna be mad. You've been**
34   **leeching off them all these years.** *(NORMAN laughs like a*
35   *hyena.)*

1 LANCE: Would you stop that? You keep talking like that, and
2 you're never gonna score.
3 NORMAN: Lance, you're not listening to me. I'm not trying to
4 score. We're just friends.
5 LANCE: Norman, no girl wants to be just friends.
6 NORMAN: They don't?
7 LANCE: No. Haven't you ever seen a Madonna video? Take it
8 from an expert. Women are just putty in a man's hands. Oh,
9 sure, they don't want to admit it, but women are just putty in
10 a man's hands.
11 NORMAN: I don't know, Lance. What about relationships? When
12 all you're after is selfish conquests, how can you experience
13 honest interaction?
14 LANCE: That's what I'm talking about, a little honest interaction.
15 Now come on, tell the truth: Who's the lucky victim tonight?
16 NORMAN: Well, it's the craziest thing.
17 LANCE: Yeah, yeah, it always is ... come on.
18 NORMAN: I'm here with Wendy ... your sister.
19 LANCE: My sister? Get out of the car, Norman. You're trying to
20 score with my sister. I'm gonna kill you. *(They both exit the car.*
21 *LANCE starts choking NORMAN.)*
22 NORMAN: *(Yelling)* Duke, Duke, he's over here. *(Both run off.)*
23
24
25
26
27
28
29
30
31
32
33
34
35

Leave It to Squirrellie — Stuck with Freddie

By Dan Rupple and Dave Toole

Cast: Announcer, Freddie, Squirrellie, Jane, Warren.

Setting: Warren's office building. The elevator is pantomimed. You may make a "Please Use the Stairs" sign.

Props: None.

Costumes: Fifties-type attire for all. Jane should wear a dress, heels, pearls and an apron. Warren wears a suit. The boys should dress casually.

1   **ANNOUNCER:** *(From Off-stage)* ***Leave It to Squirrellie****,* **with Hugh**
2   **Budford, Barbara Billingsworth, Tommy Dow and Jerry**
3   **Smathers — he's Squirrellie.** *(Enter SQUIRRELLIE and*
4   *FREDDIE.)*
5   **FREDDIE: Come on, Squirrellie, we're late.**
6   **SQUIRRELLIE: Well, I'm coming. Gee, Freddie, this is really**
7   **neat. Family Day at my dad's office.**
8   **FREDDIE: Ah, it's no big deal. I've seen lots of offices in my day.**
9   **C'mon, let's get upstairs. Don't want to keep the big boys**
10 **waiting.** *(SQUIRRELLIE goes the opposite direction.)* **Where ya**
11 **goin'?**
12 **SQUIRRELLIE: Back to the stairs.**
13 **FREDDIE: Stairs? The elevator's right here.**
14 **SQUIRRELLIE: Yeah, I know, but the sign says to use the stairs.**
15 **FREDDIE: That's all a scam, Sam. The bigwigs just put that there**
16 **to keep it for themselves.**
17 **SQUIRRELLIE: Well, I don't know, Freddie. My dad said not to**
18 **use it. Ona counta it might break.**
19 **FREDDIE: It might break? Hey, the radio in my car might break,**
20 **but that doesn't keep me from using it, does it? Besides, we're**
21 **in a hurry.**
22 **SQUIRRELLIE: Well, I guess it'll be all right, so long as we just go**
23 **straight up.**
24 **FREDDIE: Of course we'll go straight up. Where else ya gonna go**
25 **in an elevator? The Bahamas? Hee-hee. Third floor, and make**
26 **it snappy, James.** *(SQUIRRELLIE pantomimes pushing the*
27 *button. Elevator starts, FREDDIE sings, elevator stops.)*
28 **FREDDIE: Hey, what happened?**
29 **SQUIRRELLIE: The elevator stopped.**
30 **FREDDIE: What'd ya do, squirt?**
31 **SQUIRRELLIE: I didn't do nothin', Freddie. I just pushed the**
32 **button, that's all.**
33 **FREDDIE: I don't need your excuses. I gotta get out of here.**
34 **SQUIRRELLIE: Why, Freddie? You gotta go to the bathroom?**
35 **FREDDIE: I'm not talkin' about that. I'm talkin' about survival!**

1   We're gonna die down here.

2 SQUIRRELLIE: Gee, Freddie, do you think so?

3 FREDDIE: You know it, Sam. These elevators have a mind of their

4   own. One wrong move, we could wind up in China.

5 SQUIRRELLIE: Gee, Freddie, really?

6 FREDDIE: You gotta promise me somethin', Squirrellie. If I pass

7   out, you'll give me mouth-to-mouth resuscitation.

8 SQUIRRELLIE: Gee, Freddie, I don't know if I can do that. I

9   never kissed a guy before. I never even kissed a girl yet.

10 FREDDIE: I'm not askin' ya to kiss me, I'm askin' you to save my

11   life.

12 SQUIRRELLIE: Well, I saw Gus the fireman do it once, and it

13   looked like kissin' to me. *(The elevator starts again.)* Hey, we're

14   moving! See, squirt? I told you there was nothing to worry

15   about ... except what your old man's gonna do to you. *(They*

16   *exit the elevator. Enter WARREN and JANE.)*

17 WARREN: Hello, Squirrellie.

18 SQUIRRELLIE: Hi, Dad. Hi, Mom.

19 FREDDIE: Hello, Mr. Cheevers, Mrs. Cheevers. My, you're lookin'

20   lovely today.

21 JANE: Thank you, Freddie. Are you all right, Squirrellie? *(JANE*

22   *gives SQUIRRELLIE a big hug.)* I was so worried. *(JANE gives*

23   *SQUIRRELLIE a kiss on the cheek.)*

24 SQUIRRELLIE: Gee, Mom, you don't have to slobber on me.

25 FREDDIE: Not so fast. Better your Mom be slobberin' than your

26   Dad be clobberin'.

27 WARREN: Quiet, Freddie!

28 SQUIRRELLIE: I guess you're gonna holler at me now, huh?

29 WARREN: Well, Squirrellie, I thought I told you not to take the

30   elevator.

31 FREDDIE: Oh, we didn't take it, Mr. Cheevers. We were

32   kidnapped and thrown in there by wild Iraqis.

33 JANE: Iraqis! Oh, you poor boys.

34 WARREN: Iraqis? Do I really look that stupid?

35 SQUIRRELLIE: Yeah, well, I knew you said we shouldn't, but

1   Freddie said we should, and I said we shouldn't ona counta

2   you said we shouldn't, but he said we should ona counta we

3   were late, and I didn't want to be late, and you didn't want us

4   to be late, so ...

5   WARREN: Squirrellie, what if someone told you to steal money out

6   of my wallet? Would you do that too?

7   SQUIRRELLIE: Well, gee, Dad, I'd never do that, ona counta all

8   your money's in Mom's purse.

9   WARREN: Well, Squirrellie, I think it's time you learned that there

10   are God-given rules we have to live by, and you've got to do

11   what is right.

12   SQUIRRELLIE: And I kinda did what was wrong?

13   JANE: Squirrellie, what if something would've happened down

14   there?

15   SQUIRRELLIE: You mean, like if Freddie had died?

16   WARREN: Exactly. How would you have felt if Freddie had

17   actually died in there?

18   SQUIRRELLIE: Gee, Dad, well, not as good as you would've felt.

19   WARREN: Never mind. My point is you are responsible for your

20   actions, and you have to realize how they can affect others.

21   SQUIRRELLIE: Yeah, and how they can affect me too. I never felt

22   so creepy. You know, I'm a pretty lucky guy. I've got a pretty

23   neat mom and dad who love me even when I do goofy stuff.

24   JANE: Well, at least you're all right now. Let's all get going. Your

25   brother Willy's waiting.

26   SQUIRRELLIE: OK, Mom. *(They all exit. Optional music theme.)*

27

28

29

30

31

32

33

34

35

The Limited Offer

By Dave Toole

Cast: Spokesperson, Announcer.

Setting: TV studio.

Props: None.

Costumes: Suit and tie.

1 SPOKESPERSON: Ever notice some people are always smiling? I
2 don't mean that phony grin that you wear at work; I mean a
3 smile that tells the rest of the world they're *happy*! Well, now
4 you too can enjoy that same secret *millions* have shared and
5 enjoyed for years: Jesus Christ.
6 Yes, this miracle worker has been around a long time,
7 saving and helping thousands of lost souls just like you. And
8 now you too can enjoy the comfort of a living Savior right in
9 the privacy of your own home. This is no imitation! Many
10 others have tried to duplicate his wonderful offer, but no one
11 has even come close to the one and only original hope of
12 mankind.
13 Just listen to a few of the miracles this amazing man has
14 done for others. He's cured leprosy and palsy; he's cast out
15 demons and even conquered death. Through him you can
16 solve your marital problems, your financial problems, your
17 personal problems, *even* problems you've long since forgotten!
18 He gives, he loves, he helps, he saves and much, much more.
19 Now, you've probably seen things like this advertised on
20 TV. Things like EST, yoga, Zen, even Scientology — selling for
21 much, much more than they're worth. But send no money!
22 Just ask Jesus Christ to forgive your sins and come into your
23 heart.
24 So act today. You'll not only be saved from hell, but you'll
25 also receive, *free,* this eternal pass to the beautiful kingdom of
26 heaven. Yes, you too can live in the city of gold streets and
27 have your name joyously inscribed in the Lamb's Book of
28 Life. So call today. Just dial GOD-TO-DAY. That's GOD-TO-
29 DAY. If it's long distance, call collect. But act today; this offer
30 is limited!
31 ANNOUNCER: *(From Off-stage)* If you were unable to reach God
32 earlier, please try again. Operators are standing by.
33
34
35

46

Lucifer Son Shield

By Dan Rupple

Cast: Monty Lucifer.

Setting: A TV commercial on location at a lab.

Props: Red bottle (or clear one containing red food coloring and water mixture) with label reading "Lucifer Son Shield."

Costumes: A dark (preferably black) suit, shirt and tie.

1   *(Suggested song, "School's Out," [from Alice Cooper's album by*
2   *the same name, Warner Bros., 1972]. As the music fades, MONTY*
3   *LUCIFER enters.)*
4   MONTY LUCIFER: That's right, school's out. And that means
5   more free time for you. Time for fun, frolic and adventure.
6   Time for searching, seeking and trying new things. But in the
7   heat of summer, beware! Too many carefree coeds get
8   overwhelmed by the Son's enlightening rays. That's why I'm
9   here. Hi, I'm Monty Lucifer. I *care* about your soul, and I
10 know what can happen to it when you expose it to the Son. So
11 *I've* done something about it. My scientists here at Down-
12 Below Laboratories have developed all-new Lucifer Son
13 Shield Lotion. That's right, the one in the red bottle. Sure,
14 many have tried others: drug lotions, sex lotions, occult
15 lotions. But when you come right down to it, it's all the same
16 formula. So why not use the original? *And* only Lucifer Son
17 Shield is all-weather. That's right, you can wear it any time.
18 Wear it in the snow, wear it in the rain, wear it to church, wear
19 it to bed, just wear it. You never know when the Son will pop
20 out. So be ready to fight off his powerful rays. We here at
21 Down-Below Laboratories will do anything to keep you from
22 the Son. Lucifer Son Shield Lotion. Don't go anywhere
23 without it.
24
25
26
27
28
29
30
31
32
33
34
35

Montague — The Practical Joker

By Dan Rupple and Dave Toole

Cast: Announcer, Phil Montague, Clyde Bowers, Caller #1, Caller #2.

Setting: A TV Talk show. Two chairs are at Center Stage, angling in toward each other.

Props: A clipped magazine ad.

Costumes: Phil Montague wears big glasses, a white or gray hairpiece and a suit and tie. Clyde Bowers should be dressed all in black.

Sound Effects: Optional theme music.

1　ANNOUNCER: *(From Off-stage)* **And now, live, America's foremost**
2　**audience participation talk show, *Montague*. And here's your**
3　**host, Phil Montague.**
4　**PIIIL: Thank you, thank you.** *(Moving into the audience)* **Ummm,**
5　**would you please indicate with your applause which of the**
6　**following statements you agree with? First, I believe I have as**
7　**much of a sense of humor as the next guy, but with comedy, as**
8　**with anything else, it has a time and a place.** *(Pause.)* **OK, how**
9　**about the statement "Anything for a laugh?"** *(Pause.)* **All right,**
10　**I have here an ad** *(Holds it up)* **clipped out of the back of a**
11　**national tabloid that reads, "Fatal can be fun. Lethal practical**
12　**jokes performed for reasonable fees." Then there's a number**
13　**here for more information, and then in bold type it says, "He**
14　**who laughs last, laughs best!"** *(CLYDE enters.)* **With us today**
15　**is Mr. Clyde Bowers.** *(PHIL and CLYDE sit.)* **Mr. Bowers would**
16　**have you know that he feels that anything that makes you**
17　**laugh is OK, and in fact, the more serious the consequences,**
18　**the funnier the joke. Mr. Bowers is a lethal practical joker. Mr.**
19　**Bowers, could you explain to us what it is you do?**
20　**CLYDE: Sure, Phil. You know, I enjoy a good laugh at another's**
21　**expense. I think everyone does. Difference being I make sure**
22　**it's a good laugh by making sure my fall guy — that's the**
23　**technical term, Phil — buys it, and buys it big!**
24　**PHIL: Then if I'm hearing you correctly, you're talking about**
25　**slipping on a banana peel or a pie in the face, right?**
26　**CLYDE: Right, Phil, but let's go a step further. Let's take that same**
27　**pie, but this time let's slip in a live hand grenade! Now we're**
28　**talking funny — real funny!**
29　**PHIL: So what sets you apart from most practical jokers is in your**
30　**case, people could get hurt or even die!**
31　**CLYDE: Not could die, got to die. That's the beauty of it.**
32　**PHIL: Our guest today is Mr. Clyde Bowers; our topic, lethal**
33　**practical jokes. We hope you'll stay with us. Now Clyde, let's**
34　**get more specific. Could you give us some examples of what it**
35　**is you do?**

1 CLYDE: Glad to. One of my favorites is the old laughing gas in the
2   diving tanks. They get down there about a hundred feet or so
3   and just laugh themselves to death. They get all bug-eyed,
4   bubbles everywhere, hilarious! The fish love it too! Great way
5   to go! There's another one that's kind of funny — the old
6   nitroglycerin in the whoopy cushion. *Pfft-boom!* Quite an
7   eruption, as well as a surprise! You talk about your nuclear
8   waste!
9 PHIL: And you laugh at this?
10 CLYDE: Sure, sure. Look, Phil, it's a natural fact — people love to
11   laugh at the misfortunes of others.
12 PHIL: But Clyde, why kill people?
13 CLYDE: Because it's the ultimate. Comedy has always been used to
14   put people in their place, and where's the ultimate place? Six
15   feet under, and that's where I put them!
16 PHIL: Mr. Bowers, how do you pick your targets?
17 CLYDE: You know, Phil, it's not as hard as you might think. Potential
18   victims are everywhere. The rude waitress who won't fill your
19   coffee cup, the guy with the Trans-Am that takes up two
20   parking spaces or just the yahoo that insults your intelligence.
21 PHIL: You mean you'd actually kill someone for just one slip-up?
22 CLYDE: You bet your life.
23 PHIL: Listen, Clyde, do you have any friends? I mean, can *anyone*
24   trust you?
25 CLYDE: I think people trust me. Why, just two years ago my
26   neighbor, Ed Beasley, lent me his lawn mower.
27 PHIL: But Clyde, I'm not talking about lawn mowers; I'm talking
28   about trusting relationships. If we can't trust our neighbors,
29   who can we trust? I think we're left with a cold, impersonal
30   society. Is the caller there?
31 CALLER #1: *(From Off-stage)* I just want to agree with what you're
32   saying, Phil. I live in Mr. Bowers' neighborhood, and I have to tell
33   you, it's the most depressing, frightening situation imaginable. We
34   are literally hostages in our own home. My kids haven't been
35   outside for two years. No one in the neighborhood trusts him

1   … except for the late Ed Beasley.
2   CLYDE: Is this Bob Hogan?
3   CALLER #1: Uh, uh …
4   CLYDE: It is, isn't it? *(CALLER #1 hangs up.)*
5   PHIL: Now, did he just make the list?
6   CLYDE: Well, let's just say if I were him, I wouldn't use my Water
7   Pik® next week! *(Laughs.)*
8   PHIL: Isn't there something sick about hurting people for fun? I
9   mean, isn't laughing at someone's death degrading, or at least
10   lowering the value of life itself?
11   CLYDE: Oh sure, if you believe that human life has value.
12   Personally, I don't believe that. I mean, this concept of an
13   imaginary God or some pre-ordained purpose? Nah! Eat,
14   drink and be merry, for — how's that phrase go? Tomorrow
15   we die. Especially in my neighborhood!
16   PHIL: Is the caller there?
17   CALLER #2: Yes, Mr. Bowers, I was wondering, doesn't your
18   conscience bother you?
19   CLYDE: No, not at all. I don't believe there's anything wrong with
20   what I do.
21   CALLER #2: But where do you get these beliefs? I mean, what's
22   right and what's wrong? Do we believe the Bible? Or do we
23   believe mythology, or fairy tales — or even *Cosmopolitan*?
24   CLYDE: Well, I think you've got to base your beliefs on a little of
25   everything. Lately, I've been getting a lot out of Top Forty
26   radio. Like that Michael Jackson song, "Beat It." That's good
27   stuff! And those other fellas, "Whip It." And how do they
28   "Whip It?" They "Whip It" *good!*
29   PHIL: Well, regardless of how they do it, we're out of time. Mr.
30   Bowers, thank you for being with us, and thank you ladies and
31   gentlemen, for your questions and your opinions.
32   ANNOUNCER: *(From Off-stage)* You've been watching *The Phil
33   Montague Show*, brought to you by Miss Clearhold hair spray —
34   hair spray of the stars. Marlo uses it, and so does Phil.
35   *(Optional theme music plays.)*

P-R-A-Y-E-R

By Dan Rupple

Cast: Announcer; Persons 1, 2, 3, 4.

Setting: The set of a television commercial.

Props: None.

Costumes: Casual attire for all.

1   *(PERSONS 1, 2 and 3 stand at Center Stage.)*
2   **ANNOUNCER:** *(From Off-stage)* **How do you spell relief?**
3   **PERSON 1: I spell relief P-R-A-Y-E-R.**
4   **PERSON 2: How do I spell relief? I spell it P-R-A-Y-E-R.**
5   **PERSON 3: Uh-oh! I spell relief P-R-A-Y-E-R.**
6   **ANNOUNCER: That's right, prayer, for fast relief.**
7   **Are the pressures of this old world getting to you? No**
8   **matter how hard you try, you just can't find peace. Well, why**
9   **put up with worries, doubts and fears when relief is just a**
10   **prayer away? "Cast your cares upon him, because he cares for**
11   **you"** (1 Peter 5:7, author's paraphrase). **Allow the peace that**
12   **passes all understanding to keep your heart and your mind**
13   (Philippians 4:7)**. That's right — your mind also. So don't just**
14   **say "so long" to that nervous stomach, but "bye-bye" to those**
15   **migraines, too. It's not new, it's always been there. Just ask for**
16   **it in Jesus' name.** *(PERSON 4 enters.)*
17   **PERSON 4: How do I spell relief? I used to spell it I-M-P-O-S-S-I-**
18   **B-L-E, but now I spell it P-R-A-Y-E-R.**
19   **ANNOUNCER: Prayer. In spirit and in truth.**
20
21
22
23
24
25
26
27
28
29
30
31
32
33
34
35

Rapture Airlines

By Dan Rupple

Cast: Announcer.

Setting: None. (Audio-only sketch.)

Props: None.

Costumes: None.

1	**ANNOUNCER:** *(From Off-stage)* **Having trouble planning that**
2	**next vacation? Famous world sights getting humdrum? Are**
3	**you tired of hotels, coffee shops and cranky flight attendants?**
4	**Then why not take the eternal vacation? That's right, Rapture**
5	**Airlines! You don't even have to go to the airport. No, Rapture**
6	**Airlines is taking off right from where you stand. And your**
7	**flight — oh boy, plenty of leg space, music by the archangel**
8	**and complimentary glasses of living water. And that's just the**
9	**start. When you arrive at your destination, there's no waiting**
10	**in a crummy hotel lobby. The owner himself will be there to**
11	**greet you with the keys to your own private mansion. It's so**
12	**beautiful, you'll think you're in heaven. Well, you are. So**
13	**don't put if off. Get your name written in the Book of Life**
14	**today. We could take off at any time. Don't get caught up in**
15	**the world. Get caught up in Rapture Airlines — truly the *only***
16	***way* to fly.**
17	
18	
19	
20	
21	
22	
23	
24	
25	
26	
27	
28	
29	
30	
31	
32	
33	
34	
35	

Rapture Hotlines 1, 2 and 3

By Dan Rupple and Larry Watt

Cast: Man, Rapture Hotline.

Setting: Man's home.

Props: A telephone.

Costumes: Casual clothes.

Sound Effects: Ringing telephone.

1 *(MAN enters and picks up telephone.)*
2 **MAN: Think I'll call that rapture line, see if the Christians are still**
3   **around.** *(Dials ... Rings ... Answer.)*
4 **RAPTURE HOTLINE:** *(From Off-stage)* **Hello, Rapture Hotline.**
5   **Can I help you?**
6 **MAN: Uh, yeah, I just wanted to make sure all the Christians were**
7   **still around.**
8 **RAPTURE HOTLINE: Yes, we are. Were you interested in**
9   **accepting Jesus Christ as your Lord and Savior?**
10 **MAN: Well, I gotta get to a party. I'll think about it later.** *(Hangs*
11   *up and exits.)*
12
13   ********************
14
15 *(MAN enters and picks up telephone.)*
16 **MAN: Think I'll give those Christians another call down at**
17   **Rapture Hotline. Ha, ha!** *(Dials ... Rings ... Answer.)*
18 **RAPTURE HOTLINE: Hello, Rapture Hotline.**
19 **MAN: Uh, yeah, I just wanted to make sure you Christians were**
20   **still there.**
21 **RAPTURE HOTLINE: We sure are. Were you interested in**
22   **accepting Jesus as your Lord and Savior?**
23 **MAN: Uh, I'll have to think about it some more. I've got to get**
24   **down to the beach and catch some rays. Uh, see ya later.**
25   *(Hangs up and exits.)*
26
27   ********************
28
29 *(MAN enters and picks up telephone.)*
30 **MAN: One more time for Rapture Hotline.** *(Dials ... Rings ... And*
31   *rings ... MAN exits, panicked.)*
32
33
34
35

The Return of Christ

By Dan Rupple

Cast: Announcer, Onlookers (two or more), Captain, Lieutenant, Corporal.

Setting: A movie set.

Props: None.

Costumes: Costumes from various parts of the world for the Onlookers. Fatigues or military uniforms for the Platoon.

Sound Effects: Gunfire, crashing noise.

1   *(ONLOOKERS stand at Center Stage, pointing up and gesturing*
2   *while music plays.)*
3   **ANNOUNCER: You remember the original! It changed the world!**
4   **Now Last Supper Productions presents the long-awaited**
5   **sequel, *The Return of Christ.* (Music) Yes, never before has**
6   **there been a spectacle such as this. The whole world is waiting.**
7   **The stage is set. What about you? Are you ready for the return**
8   **of Christ?** *(ONLOOKERS exit. Option: Insert* Rapture Hotline #3
9   *[page 58] here.)* **The Return of Christ, with a story so**
10   **intriguing, you could get caught up in it. It's coming soon to**
11   **your city.** *(The PLATOON runs On-stage as gunfire sounds are*
12   *heard.)*
13   **CAPTAIN: You men over there, secure that wall. We've got to keep**
14   **him from coming through that gate.**
15   **LIEUTENANT: Don't worry, Captain. No one could open that**
16   **gate. It's been closed for a couple thousand years.**
17   **CORPORAL:** *(Pointing)* **Captain! Captain! He's coming, and he's**
18   **got a huge army with him.**
19   **CAPTAIN: Battle stations! Battle stations! Be brave, men. We can**
20   **win this thing.** *(A crash is heard.)* **How about the best two out**
21   **of three?** *(Music as PLATOON pantomimes.)*
22   **ANNOUNCER: No matter what you do, you cannot miss the**
23   **triumphant return of Jesus Christ, coming in all his power**
24   **and glory. When you hear the horses gallop, make sure you're**
25   **riding with the leader of the pack. *The Return of Christ.* We**
26   **urge you, believe it before you see it!**
27
28
29
30
31
32
33
34
35

Spouse's Super Bout

By Dan Rupple

Cast: Announcers — Len Summers, Jeff Mullins; Spouses — Walt and Linda Donaldson.

Setting: Live television coverage from the Donaldson kitchen. Stage Right is the kitchen area, which may be imaginary or something as simple as a card table on which Linda may do her "work." For a fun touch, put up some goal posts. The "broadcast booth" at Stage Left may be two chairs side by side with a table in front and two phone headsets or microphones for the announcers.

Props: A bowl and spoon for Linda, papers on the table of the broadcast booth, something for Walt to throw that will make a lot of noise.

Costumes: Suits and ties for Len, Jeff and Walt. Linda should wear casual clothes.

Notes: Crowd noise may be taped. This sketch was written in 1983, when the price of golf clubs was less than a microwave. Since that's no longer true, feel free to substitute other items.

1	(*LEN and JEFF are in the broadcast booth at Stage Left. LINDA is*
2	*in the kitchen at Stage Right. She freezes until her action begins.*)
3	LEN: Hello, and welcome to the sporting event of the year: the
4	Spouse's Super Bout. I'm Len Summers. Along with me here
5	in the booth is our commentator, Jeff Mullins. Jeff, I'm
6	looking for quite a contest today.
7	JEFF: That's right, Len. You don't get to the Super Bout without
8	being the best, and that is certainly the case in today's
9	matchup.
10	LEN: For the Midwest Husbands, a ten-year pro, at the peak of his
11	career, Walt Donaldson. And the challenger, for the Pacific
12	Coast Wives, just recently coming into her own, Linda
13	Donaldson.
14	JEFF: These two couldn't be better matched, Len. In Walt we have
15	toughness and strong reasoning abilities, and with Linda
16	we're going to see those ever-mounting emotions along with
17	verbal quickness. It's going to be a real battle.
18	LEN: Well, we're excited to be here, and we're glad you could join
19	us. The game's about to begin. Let's go down to the field for
20	the opening kickoff. (*LINDA unfreezes and begins humming and*
21	*cooking in the kitchen.*) Linda opens. Right now she's calm and
22	seemingly very peaceful.
23	JEFF: Len, she's either suppressing or just trying to establish the
24	pace. (*Enter WALT from work.*)
25	WALT: Hi, honey.
26	LINDA: Hi, Walt.
27	WALT: When's dinner?
28	LINDA: In about an hour.
29	WALT: An hour? Why so late?
30	LINDA: Hey, dinner doesn't just magically appear. It takes time.
31	LEN: Good sarcasm by Linda.
32	JEFF: She's always been a master.
33	WALT: Why didn't you start earlier?
34	LINDA: I've been busy!
35	WALT: Busy? Doing what?

1   LINDA: I had to ...

2   WALT: Obviously not fixing up the house. How can you sit around

3   all day in this mess? *(Crowd roars.)*

4   LEN: Oooo, there we have it. The first real attack of the game.

5   JEFF: Walt does a fabulous move here. He does a double

6   maneuver. First he interrupts, then he makes an insult about

7   Linda's housekeeping, which changes the subject.

8   LEN: Let's look at that again on instant replay.

9   WALT: Busy? Doing what?

10   LEN: A little bite there.

11   LINDA: I had to ...

12   WALT: Obviously not fixing up the house.

13   JEFF: There it is, Len. He gives Linda no time to respond.

14   WALT: How can you sit around all day in this mess?

15   JEFF: This shows Walt's experience. He attacks her housekeeping

16   and her laziness — all in the same statement.

17   LEN: Let's return to live action.

18   LINDA: Sit around all day? Is that what you think? I suppose a

19   dwarf comes in at night and cleans your socks.

20   LEN: Once again, good sarcasm by Linda.

21   WALT: Very funny. Well, if I'm going to have to wait for my

22   dinner, I might as well read the paper. Where is it?

23   LINDA: It's still out in the yard. I forgot to get it.

24   WALT: Forgot to get it? Do you ever get it?

25   LINDA: I get it all the time.

26   WALT: When? You never go out and get it. I always have to get it.

27   LEN: Oh, what aggression. Walt is scoring big.

28   JEFF: Len, Walt is a pro, that's all there is to it. Let's see it again.

29   WALT: Very funny. Well, if I'm going to have to wait for my

30   dinner, I might as well read the paper ...

31   JEFF: Now this is brilliant. He's setting her up. Walt knows very

32   well that she hasn't brought the paper in. This play is known

33   as "rubbing it in."

34   LINDA: I get it all the time.

35   JEFF: Now, Linda is vulnerable here. She's on the defense.

1 WALT: You never go out and get it. I always have to get it.

2 JEFF: Here's another tactic: gross exaggeration. He uses the

3   words *never* and *always*. It's quite effective, and Walt executes

4   it well.

5 LEN: Walt's really on a streak. Linda better act soon, or she may

6   have to wait until next year. Let's return to live action.

7 LINDA: Well, maybe your mother should move in with us. Then

8   you'd have your paper and your dinner on time. *(Groan from*

9   *crowd)*

10 WALT: Don't bring my mother into this.

11 LINDA: Why not? You already brought her into our marriage!

12   *(Crowd roars.)*

13 LEN: Oh, Linda scores.

14 JEFF: Just when we counted Linda out, she comes back once again

15   with sarcasm. As I said before, it's her strength, and when it's

16   applied to family, it can be deadly. I'm not sure Walt can come

17   back after that. It was devastating.

18 WALT: Look, you're making this whole thing into a fight. I just

19   wanted to know when we were having dinner.

20 LEN: Walt's trying to regain control.

21 LINDA: Well, maybe if you would buy me a microwave oven,

22   dinner would be ready.

23 WALT: We can't afford a microwave.

24 LINDA: Well, Walter, we were able to afford those golf clubs last

25   summer.

26 WALT: Golf clubs are a little cheaper than a microwave.

27 LINDA: George bought Carol a microwave.

28 JEFF: We're seeing a lot of mind games here. Both parties are

29   using comparisons and insinuations and recalling past fights.

30   Tension is definitely mounting.

31 LEN: And notice that Linda called Walt "Walter." That's a good

32   play.

33 WALT: Are you saying you'd rather be married to George? *(Pause)*

34   Huh? *(Pause)* Come on, would you? *(Silence, then "Ahhhh"*

35   *from crowd)*

1　LEN:　This is great. Linda gives him the silent treatment.

2　JEFF:　Emotions are her most potent weapons. I knew it was just a
3　　　　matter of time before we saw them.

4　WALT:　Look, drop the whole thing. You're upset.

5　LINDA:　Who's upset? I'm not upset!

6　JEFF:　Linda goes into emotional denial. Looks like she'll score
7　　　　again.

8　WALT:　Well, if you're not upset, maybe you will be now! *(WALT*
9　　　　*throws an object on the floor.)*

10　JEFF:　Oh, Walt's back in the game. He counters with physical
11　　　　tantrums.

12　LEN:　Linda's in a corner now. *(Silent pause)* A hush falls over the
13　　　　crowd. *(Outburst of crying from LINDA. Crowd roars.)* I don't
14　　　　believe it! Uncontrollable crying! And Linda scores!

15　JEFF:　The crowd loves it, Len. Linda's crying has totally disarmed
16　　　　Walt.

17　LEN:　Can Walt pull victory out of sure defeat?

18　WALT:　Honey, I'm sorry. Look — I'm tired, and I'm taking it all
19　　　　out on you.

20　LINDA:　No, I'm sorry. I'm being childish.

21　WALT:　Let's go into the den and talk about it. Dinner can wait.

22　LINDA:　OK. *(Roar from crowd)*

23　LEN:　It's over! The marriage wins!

24　JEFF:　Len, this has been a great match. I was sure, with the way
25　　　　they were going at it, that the marriage would lose, but we
26　　　　have a victory, and the crowd loves it!

27　LEN:　Let's see that thrilling victory again.

28　WALT:　Honey, I'm sorry. Look — I'm tired, and I'm taking it all
29　　　　out on you.

30　JEFF:　This is great. Walt apologizes and verbalizes the source of
31　　　　the argument.

32　LINDA:　No, I'm sorry. I'm being childish.

33　JEFF:　Here's a crucial play. Linda *also* apologizes, but then she
34　　　　doesn't counter with blame. Instead, she admits a bad
35　　　　reaction to the situation on her part.

1   **LEN: And they both walk away winners. Well, that's it from the**
2   **Spouse's Super Bout. Hope you enjoyed it as much as we did.**
3   **This is Len Summers along with Jeff Mullins. Thanks for**
4   **joining us.**
5
6
7
8
9
10
11
12
13
14
15
16
17
18
19
20
21
22
23
24
25
26
27
28
29
30
31
32
33
34
35

Stooges Three and the Lion's Den

By Dave Toole

Cast: Moab, Curley Josephus, Larriticus, Daniel, Maccabees (Mac for short).

Setting: Bible times. Stage Right is the table where they roll dice and also sleep later. You may put some large potted plants in this area to obscure Moab, Curley Josephus and Larriticus as they sleep. This also obscures the fact that Moab is beating up the air and not a real lion! Stage Left is the "lion's cage" area.

Props: Dice, a lion's head, a sign reading "Dawn of the Next Day," "lion skins" (may be made of furry fabric available in fabric stores), and a jar labeled "Sleeping Manna."

Costumes: Thirties-era clothing: pants with suspenders, suits, hats, etc. If you can find wigs, Moab may wear a black "bowl cut" and Larriticus may wear a long, curly wig. Or you could mix and match from the thirties and biblical times, for example, a robe, sandals, and bowl-cut wig for Moab.

Sound Effects: Dice rattling in a cup and falling onto the table, boinks and slaps, coconuts hitting together, lion roars, rooster crow, female voices, low grumble, keys rattling in a lock, iron door slamming.

Notes: To get the full comic effect, watch The Three Stooges' film shorts until you can imitate their physical humor well. There are several Web sites devoted to those three knuckleheads that you can look at for inspiration.

1   *(CURLEY JOSEPHUS and MOAB sit at a table. The sound of*
2   *dice rattling in a cup [actually CURLEY JOSEPHUS' mouth] is*
3   *heard.)*

4   **MOAB: C'mon, lunkhead, spit out them dice.**

5   **CURLEY JOSEPHUS:** *(With his mouth full)* **C'mon, baby. Daddy**
6   **needs a new pair of sandals.** *(The "rattling" sound effect is*
7   *heard, and then CURLEY JOSEPHUS spits out the dice. They*
8   *tumble.)*

9   **MOAB: Ewww, they're all wet!**

10   **CURLEY JOSEPHUS: Yeah, but look — seven! Yuk, yuk, yuk.**

11   **MOAB: I'll show you seven. Here's two** *(Boink)* **and five makes**
12   **seven.** *(Slap. Enter LARRITICUS.)*

13   **LARRITICUS: Moab, Curley Josephus.**

14   **CURLEY JOSEPHUS: Hail, Larriticus. What message bearest**
15   **thou?**

16   **LARRITICUS: What?**

17   **MOAB: He means, "What's the matter?"** *(To CURLEY JOSEPHUS.*
18   *Slap, boink)* **What message bearest thou?!**

19   **LARRITICUS: Oh, it's our master, Daniel. He wouldn't bow**
20   **before the King's idol. They're going to feed him to the lions**
21   **in the morning.**

22   **CURLY JOSEPHUS: What do we do, Moab?**

23   **MOAB: We gotta put our heads together.** *(The sound of coconuts*
24   *knocking together is heard as they do so.)*

25   **CURLEY JOSEPHUS, MOAB and LARRITICUS:** *(Stumbling*
26   *back and holding their heads)* **Ouch!**

27   **MOAB: C'mon, you guys! We need a plan!**

28   **LARRITICUS: Yeah, a plan!**

29   **CURLEY JOSEPHUS: Sure, a plan!** *(Each Stooge sings one note of*
30   *a three-part chord, e.g., C-E-G.)*

31   **MOAB:** *(Singing the low note)* **A plan …**

32   **LARRITICUS:** *(Singing the middle note)* **A plan …**

33   **CURLEY JOSEPHUS:** *(Singing the high note)* **A plan …**

34   **MOAB, LARRITICUS and CURLEY JOSEPHUS:** *(Singing together*
35   *in harmony)* **A plan!**

1   **MOAB: All right, here's what we do ...** *(They exit Stage Right while*
2   *talking. A stagehand may remove the table. After a pause, they*
3   *reenter Stage Left, the "lion's cage" area. Assorted lion roars are*
4   *heard.)*
5   **CURLEY JOSEPHUS: Hey Moab, you sure Maccabees still keeps**
6   **the lions?**
7   **MOAB: Am I sure?** *(Bonk, boink)* **Of course I'm sure.**
8   **LARRITICUS: Boy, this place sure gives me the creeps!**
9   **MOAB: I'll give you the creeps.** *(Slap, bonk)*
10   **CURLEY JOSEPHUS:** *(Looks Off-stage Right.)* **Hey, there he is.**
11   **Hey, Mac!** *(MAC enters.)*
12   **MAC: Larriticus, Moab, Curley Josephus. I wondered if you'd be**
13   **here. Daniel has been sentenced to the lion's den tomorrow**
14   **morning. He'll be taking a permanent "dirt nap."** *(A huge lion*
15   *roar is heard.)*
16   **CURLEY JOSEPHUS: Whoa, whoa, whoa, whoa, whoa.**
17   **MOAB: Hey, cut it out. What are you, a scaredy cat?**
18   **CURLEY JOSEPHUS: That's right, Moab. Scared of de cat! Yuk,**
19   **yuk, yuk.**
20   **MAC: That was Shaft, the biggest, meanest, hungriest mama lion ...**
21   **FEMALE VOICES:** *(Off-Stage)* **Shut your mouth!**
22   **MAC: I'm just talkin' 'bout Shaft. She's the baddest lion we got!**
23   **She ain't been fed for three weeks, but tomorrow, she's eatin'**
24   **kosher.**
25   **CURLY JOSEPHUS:** *(He has put on a lion's head so his voice is*
26   *muffled.)* **Hey guys, look at me. Rrrooaarrr!**
27   **LARRITICUS: Ahhh! Help!**
28   **CURLEY JOSEPHUS:** *(Taking the lion's head off)* **Don't worry, it's**
29   **only me.**
30   **MOAB: Why, you ...** *(Bam, pow)*
31   **CURLEY JOSEPHUS: Oh, a wise guy, eh? Ruff, ruff.**
32   **MOAB: Cut it out.** *(Slap, slap, anvil)* **Hey, wait a minute.** *(Points to*
33   *"skins.")* **Listen, Mac, what do you use these old lion skins for,**
34   **anyway?**
35   **MAC: Well, we put them on if we have to go into the cage.**

1   **CURLEY JOSEPHUS: In with the lions?**
2   **MAC: Well, first we give them this knock-out manna.** *(Holds up*
3   *manna jar.)*
4   **MOAB: Hey! What if we slip the real lions some of that stuff and**
5   **then put on the skins ourselves, so in the morning ...** *(They exit*
6   *Stage Right, talking. A stagehand holds up a sign saying, "Dawn*
7   *of the Next Day." MOAB, LARRITICUS and CURLEY*
8   *JOSEPHUS reenter and lie on the floor in this order: MOAB on*
9   *the end closest to Stage Left, LARRITICUS in the middle and*
10   *CURLEY JOSEPHUS on the end closest to Stage Right. A*
11   *rooster's crowing is heard.)*
12 **MOAB: Snore ...**
13 **LARRITICUS: Sigh ...**
14 **CURLEY JOSEPHUS: Whinney ...** *(A low grumble is heard. Repeat*
15   *the sequence three times ending with the low grumble.)*
16 **MOAB:** *(Waking and sitting up)* **Hey,** *(Slap)* **cut it out.** *(He slaps the*
17   *space beside him.)*
18 **LARRITICUS:** *(Sits up.)* **What?**
19 **MOAB: Your stomach's growling.**
20 **LARRITICUS: Not me.**
21 **MOAB: Oh yeah? Well, it must be Curley Josephus. Hey,**
22   **knucklehead,** *(Coconut sound as MOAB bonks space beside him)*
23   **wake up and cut it out.** *(CURLEY JOSEPHUS continues to*
24   *snore and rumble.)* **Oh, a hard case, eh? Well, let's see you sleep**
25   **through this** *(Bonk)***, or this** *(Bam)***, or this.** *(Bong)*
26 **CURLEY JOSEPHUS: Hey, Moab, whatcha doin'?**
27 **MOAB: I'm wakin' you up, you ignoramus.** *(More sound effects)*
28 **CURLEY JOSEPHUS:** *(Sits up.)* **But Moab, that ain't me. I'm over**
29   **here.**
30 **MOAB:** *(Bam)* **Oh, yeah?** *(Smack)* **Well, if you're over there, and**
31   **I'm over here, who is this?** *(A huge roar is heard.)*
32 **CURLEY JOSEPHUS, MOAB and LARRITICUS:** *(Together)*
33   **Shaft!** *(They all run around the stage with the imaginary lion*
34   *close behind.)*
35 **MOAB: C'mon, fellas, there's the keys.** *(CURLEY JOSEPHUS,*

70

1   *MOAB and LARRITICUS run Off-stage Right. The sound of keys*
2   *rattling in the lock is heard and all reenter at Stage Right with*
3   *DANIEL. An iron door opens and slams shut. A lion's roar is*
4   *heard.)*
5   **CURLEY JOSEPHUS: Whoa! Look who I ran into! Daniel!**
6   **DANIEL: Hey, what were you guys doing in there?**
7   **CURLEY JOSEPHUS: Feedin' the animals, and that ain't "lion."**
8   **Yuk, yuk, yuk.**
9   **MOAB: Quiet, lame brain!** *(Bonk)* **We thought we could help you**
10   **out.**
11   **CURLEY JOSEPHUS: Yeah, but someone must've given us the**
12   **sleepin' manna by mistake.**
13   **DANIEL: Guys, I appreciate the effort, but I thought I told you**
14   **before that God would take care of me.**
15   **MOAB: Yeah, you numbskulls!** *(Assorted physical sound effects.*
16   *LARRITICUS and CURLEY JOSEPHUS react.)* **C'mon, let's get**
17   **out of here.** *(Points Off-stage Left.)* **Open that door.**
18   **CURLEY JOSEPHUS: But Moab, that's the door to the …**
19   **MOAB: Gangway. Outta the way. I'll handle this.** *(MOAB goes Off-*
20   *stage Left. The sound of a key rattling in a lock, an iron door*
21   *opening, and a lion's roar are heard. All react as the imaginary*
22   *lion chases them around the stage as "Three Blind Mice" is*
23   *played. They exit, running.)*
24
25
26
27
28
29
30
31
32
33
34
35

The Test

By Dan Rupple

Cast: Announcer, Off-stage Voice.

Setting: Judgment Day. Optional: Place a fog machine at Center Stage.

Props: None.

Costumes: None.

Sound Effects: Recorded beep as heard in TV tests; various noises as items are loaded; loud boom.

1   ANNOUNCER: *(From Off-stage)* **This is a test. For the next sixty**
2   **seconds, each Christian's works will be tested with fire. As all**
3   **of the works of their lives are burned, their sincere motives**
4   **will be made evident. Only those works done with Jesus**
5   **Christ as the foundation will remain. Remember, this is only**
6   **a test.** *(Drawn-out beep sounds as OFF-STAGE VOICE is heard*
7   *in the background.)*
8   **OFF-STAGE VOICE: OK, load his bank account on there.** *(Loud*
9   *thud)* **Joe, you want to move over his good deeds? Do we have**
10 **the things he's done for his family?** *(Soft thud)* **All right,**
11 **everything in check? Oh, throw his church attendance and**
12 **tithes on top there.** *(Soft thud)* **Joe, the time he couldn't give**
13 **that poor man a ride to the doctor 'cause he was on his way to**
14 **the Bible study is falling off. You want to secure that?** *(Sound*
15 *of Velcro ripping)* **OK, stand back! Let 'er go!** *(Loud boom.*
16 *House lights are rapidly turned off and on. If a fog machine is*
17 *available, produce some smoke.)* **Too bad ... not much.**
18 **Someone want to sweep up those ashes? Let's get ready for**
19 **the next one.** *(Beep stops.)*
20 ANNOUNCER: **This has been a test. Had it been the real thing,**
21 **how much in your life would be remaining? Remember, this**
22 **was only a test.**
23
24
25
26
27
28
29
30
31
32
33
34
35

That's Ridiculous

By Dan Rupple

Cast: Television Hosts — John Daveedon, Katy Lee Cosboz, Stan Tareyton; Guests — Lester Purrnad, Bonnie Lindstrom and son Shawn, Dr. Ross Welby; Announcer.

Setting: The set of the television talk show, *That's Ridiculous*. Three chairs should be placed at Stage Left for the hosts. One chair should be placed at Stage Right for each guest to sit on when it is his or her turn.

Props: None.

Costumes: Lab coat for Dr. Ross Welby.

Sound Effects: Crowd noise may be taped.

1 ANNOUNCER: *(From Off-stage)* **Tonight you'll see a man who**
2 **doesn't believe that the Bible is true, a woman who thinks**
3 **Jesus was a great teacher but that he isn't God or Savior, and**
4 **a group of people who are willfully going to a place of eternal**
5 **burning and torment. It's all here tonight on …**
6 CROWD: *That's Ridiculous!*
7 ANNOUNCER: And now, let's meet the hosts of *That's Ridiculous*,
8 John Daveedon, Katy Lee Cosboz and Stan Tareyton! *(JOHN,*
9 *KATY and STAN enter and sit down.)*
10 JOHN: Thank you, and welcome to *That's Ridiculous*.
11 KATY: Tonight, as you've heard, we have another group of people
12 whose behavior, compared to normal logic, is ridiculous.
13 STAN: Our first story involves a man named Lester Purrnad from
14 Springfield, Mississippi. *(LESTER enters and sits as crowd*
15 *applauds.)* Welcome, Lester. Could you tell the audience what
16 it is that you believe?
17 LESTER: Well, sure. I believe the Bible is a bunch of fairy tales.
18 STAN: And why do you believe this?
19 LESTER: I just do. I mean, stories about a flood and man created
20 from dust and a big whale eating a man — come on!
21 STAN: Well, let's go back now. You don't believe in creationism, so
22 you must believe in evolution.
23 LESTER: I sure do. I came directly from an ape, I know it!
24 STAN: Well, the study of fossils is solidly proving that evolution is
25 false.
26 LESTER: Well, don't distort the picture with facts.
27 STAN: And archaeological discoveries have strongly supported a
28 worldwide flood estimated to have occurred during the time
29 of Noah.
30 LESTER: Really?
31 STAN: And surely, if God could create the earth and all the
32 universe, he could create a whale big enough to swallow one
33 man.
34 LESTER: Well, look, I still say someone made it all up and wrote
35 a book.

1 STAN: Well, Mr. Purrnad, the Bible isn't a book. It's sixty-six
2   books, by many different authors.
3 LESTER: It is?
4 STAN: Now, suppose you take a couple dozen people over a period
5   of a few thousand years and spread them out over about three
6   or four continents and have them write on something as
7   complex and controversial as the nature of God. What would
8   you come up with?
9 LESTER: Boy, you'd come up with something that looks like the
10   Sunday comics. Be kind of fun to read, you know, all those
11   different opinions.
12 STAN: Yes, it would, but you see, the Bible agrees with itself and
13   the nature of God.
14 LESTER: Coincidence!
15 STAN: I don't think so.
16 LESTER: Then how'd they do that?
17 STAN: Divine inspiration.
18 LESTER: No way! And even if it was true when they wrote it,
19   who's to say that what we have today is the same thing?
20 STAN: Well, manuscripts have been found dating quite a ways
21   back, and they agree totally with the manuscripts we have
22   today.
23 LESTER: Hmmm.
24 STAN: So, Mr. Purrnad, after hearing just a small portion of the
25   evidence, do you still believe the Bible is just a bunch of fairy
26   tales?
27 LESTER: You better believe it!
28 STAN: No, I think *you* had better because, Mr. Purrnad, *That's*
29   *Ridiculous! (LESTER exits. Crowd applauds.)*
30 KATY: Our next story involves a young lady from Van Nuys,
31   California, named Bonnie Lindstrom. Bonnie has a very
32   opinionated view of Jesus Christ. Let's hear her tell us what
33   she believes. *(BONNIE and SHAWN enter to applause. SHAWN*
34   *acts up while BONNIE talks.)* Bonnie, who is Jesus Christ?
35 BONNIE: Well, Jesus Christ was a man who lived two thousand

1   years ago in Nazareth — that's in Israel — and he died by
2   crucifixion.
3   KATY: And what are your views concerning this man?
4   BONNIE: Well, Katy ... may I call you Katy?
5   KATY: Yes, that would be fine.
6   BONNIE: Thank you. Well, Katy, I believe that Jesus was a
7   tremendous teacher, and as is the case with many truly great
8   men, the leaders of the day, motivated by jealousy, killed him.
9   *(Annoyed)* Shawn — settle down!
10   KATY: OK now, you believe that Jesus was a great teacher?
11   BONNIE: Most assuredly — right up there with Annie Sullivan.
12   KATY: Do you believe that Jesus is the only way to heaven?
13   BONNIE: No, I don't.
14   KATY: How about his deity? Do you believe that Jesus is God?
15   BONNIE: El negativo!
16   KATY: Well, Jesus said that he was God and that he was the only
17   way to have a relationship with God the Father.
18   BONNIE: He was probably misquoted.
19   KATY: Well, his disciples believed that, and in the Gospel of John
20   it says that Jesus called himself God, and that's why the Jews
21   wanted to kill him.
22   BONNIE: Simple misunderstanding. These things happen all the
23   time.
24   KATY: Well, Bonnie, why didn't Jesus set the record straight and
25   save his own life?
26   BONNIE: Well ... OK ... he may have said that, but I still believe
27   he was just a great teacher. Shawn, for the last time, *mellow*
28   *out!*
29   KATY: Boys will be boys.
30   BONNIE: Yes.
31   KATY: How old is Shawn?
32   BONNIE: He's seven.
33   KATY: Well, let me ask you this. If you sent him to school, and ...
34   BONNIE: Shawn goes to a private academy.
35   KATY: Yes, of course. Well, let's say that you send Shawn to the

1   academy and his teacher tells him that three plus three is five.

2   Now, no matter how good a teacher this person is, would you

3   let Shawn continue with this teacher?

4   BONNIE: Once again, Katy, el negativo to the max!

5   KATY: Why, Bonnie?

6   BONNIE: Obviously, no teacher is any good who is teaching

7   something that is contrary to the truth.

8   KATY: Then why do you believe that Jesus, who said he was

9   mankind's salvation and God, isn't Savior or God, but still a

10   great teacher?

11   BONNIE: I just do!

12   KATY: Bonnie?

13   BONNIE: Yes, Katy?

14   KATY: *That's Ridiculous! (Studio applause. BONNIE and SHAWN*

15   *exit.)*

16   JOHN: Our final story tonight is brought to us by Dr. Ross Welby,

17   who has discovered some of the most illogical behavior we

18   have ever witnessed here on *That's Ridiculous!* Let's give him

19   a warm welcome. *(DR. WELBY enters to applause and sits.)* Dr.

20   Welby, could you explain your findings?

21   DR. WELBY: Yes, John. I discovered a rather large number of

22   people who, when given the choice of eternal life in

23   unspeakable joy or eternal life in a fiery, agonizing torment,

24   will willfully choose torment.

25   JOHN: Wait a second. We're not talking about forcing them. You

26   mean a free choice?

27   DR. WELBY: Yes, they have the choice. It takes no

28   accomplishment on their part. Just a simple decision. And

29   they choose hell!

30   JOHN: You mean heck, Doctor. This is TV.

31   DR. WELBY: No, John, heck is uncomfortably warm. We're

32   talking pure hell.

33   JOHN: But is this choice clearly explained?

34   DR. WELBY: Yes, the facts are available to all, although some are

35   so determined to experience the fiery torment that they won't

1   even listen.

2   JOHN: This is hard to believe. Where are these people found?

3   DR. WELBY: Well, that's the amazing part, John. They're found

4   all over the place. You'll see them everywhere.

5   JOHN: And they choose torment over paradise?

6   DR. WELBY: Yes, that's right.

7   JOHN: Dr. Welby, *That's Ridiculous!* And that's our show for

8   tonight.

9   KATY: Hope to see you next week, but in the meantime remember ...

10   STAN: Check out what you believe, because if you don't ...

11   CROWD: *That's Ridiculous!*

12   JOHN, KATY and STAN: *(Together)* **Good night!** *(Applause)*

13

14

15

16

17

18

19

20

21

22

23

24

25

26

27

28

29

30

31

32

33

34

35

What's Gospel to You?

By Dan Rupple and Dave Toole

Cast: Clark Phillips, Val Gal, Bunky, Housewife, Businessman, Spudhead.

Setting: On the street.

Props: A microphone (optional).

Costumes: Clark and the Businessman wear suits. Val Gal and Bunky dress in trendy clothes. The Housewife dresses casually. Spudhead wears a T-shirt and jeans.

1   CLARK: Hello, I'm Clark Phillips for *Faith in Action*. I'm out here
2   on the street asking the question, "What's gospel to you?"
3   *(VAL GAL and BUNKY enter and walk toward CLARK.)* Here
4   comes a young lady. Miss, what's gospel to you?
5   VAL GAL: What's gospel to me? My boyfriend, Bunky. He's so
6   neat. I believe everything he says.
7   CLARK: You must be Bunky?
8   BUNKY: Yeah.
9   VAL GAL: See? *(VAL GAL and BUNKY exit.)*
10   CLARK: OK, moving on. *(HOUSEWIFE enters and walks toward*
11   *CLARK.)* Ma'am, what's gospel to you?
12   HOUSEWIFE: *The National Inquisitor.* The article about the UFO
13   giving Madonna a cure for cancer changed my life.
14   CLARK: Well, thank you. *(HOUSEWIFE exits. BUSINESSMAN*
15   *enters and walks toward CLARK.)* How about you, sir? What's
16   gospel to you?
17   BUSINESSMAN: Most definitely — the Dow Jones report. If they
18   make one mistake, I could be as destitute as ... well ... this
19   poor slob. *(Motions to SPUDHEAD, who has entered and started*
20   *walking toward CLARK.)*
21   SPUDHEAD: Spare a dime? *(Burps. BUSINESSMAN shakes his*
22   *head in disgust and exits.)*
23   CLARK: Here's a young gentleman. Sir, what's gospel to you?
24   SPUDHEAD: Oh, well, I don't ... Clark? Clark Phillips?
25   CLARK: Yeah, have you seen me on TV?
26   SPUDHEAD: No, it's me, Richard Menza.
27   CLARK: Spudhead?
28   SPUDHEAD: Yeah.
29   CLARK: Oh, I'm sorry, do they still call you Spudhead?
30   SPUDHEAD: Yeah. So Clark, it's been a long time. Say, do you still
31   party like a banshee?
32   CLARK: No, I've changed a lot since those days. I'm a Christian
33   now.
34   SPUDHEAD: You — a Christian? Clark Phillips?
35   CLARK: Cut the camera, Fred.

1 SPUDHEAD: The guy who drank beer through his nose?
2 CLARK: Well, yeah …
3 SPUDHEAD: The guy who buried Patty Hansen's dog up to his
4   neck in a flower bed?
5 CLARK: Well, it was a small dog.
6 SPUDHEAD: The guy who freaked out in the waterbed store with
7   an ice pick?
8 CLARK: Yeah, but I did reimburse them.
9 SPUDHEAD: I can't believe it. Fast Times Phillips fizzles out?
10   What made you do that?
11 CLARK: I was miserable, Spudhead, and I knew there was
12   something more to life.
13 SPUDHEAD: Are you kidding? What about all the fun we had?
14   Hey, those were some famous Saturday nights.
15 CLARK: Listen, Spudhead, Saturday nights don't last forever. A
16   relationship with God does.
17 SPUDHEAD: Yeah. So what are you doing out here?
18 CLARK: Well, I work with a local TV station, and I'm
19   interviewing people on the street.
20 SPUDHEAD: Great. And you want to interview me?
21 CLARK: Yeah. The question is: "What's gospel to you?"
22 SPUDHEAD: Huh?
23 CLARK: Well, Spudhead, what do you live your life by?
24 SPUDHEAD: Oh, I got a place right next to Wally's Tire
25   Warehouse.
26 CLARK: No, I mean, have you ever thought of living your life the
27   way God meant it to be lived?
28 SPUDHEAD: Gee, Clark, should I move?
29 CLARK: No! Look — can we talk? *(SPUDHEAD and CLARK*
30   *pantomime conversation as they exit.)*
31
32
33
34
35

Part 2
From the Stage

Baser Colony

By Dan Rupple

Cast: Announcer, Willis Self, M.O. Eliminator,
Abe Ortion, God.

Setting: A conference room. Place a table and three
chairs at Center Stage.

Props: A Bible.

Costumes: Business attire for all.

Sound Effects: Thunder.

1   *(WILLIS SELF, M.O. ELIMINATOR and ABE ORTION are sitting*
2   *around the table and pantomiming discussion during the opening*
3   *narration.)*
4   ANNOUNCER: *(From Off-stage)* Good evening. What you are about
5   to hear may surprise you. It may shock you. It should — it's
6   disgusting. Disgusting, but true. The rulers of the Baser
7   Colony are all in a top-secret council meeting: Secretary of
8   State Willis Self, Secretary of Defense M.O. Eliminator and
9   President Abe Ortion. These beings thrive on darkness and
10 will do anything to obtain and justify their selfish goals. Well,
11 are you ready? Let's listen in on their discussion. A word of
12 warning: Be quiet. We aren't supposed to be here, and they'd
13 just as soon kill us as look at us.
14 WILLIS: Mr. Ortion, something must be done. Baser Colony is just
15 too crowded. Overpopulation is making the food, drink and
16 pleasure rations smaller for all of us. We need a plan.
17 M.O. ELIMINATOR: Willis, Mr. Ortion is well aware of the
18 problem. That's why he's in charge — right, Abe?
19 ABE: Hmm!
20 M.O. ELIMINATOR: But Willis, this problem is much too
21 complex, much too urgent and much too important for a, well,
22 shall we say "nice and neat" little solution. We need something
23 drastic. And we need it now.
24 WILLIS: Well, obviously, M.O., we just need *fewer* people. It's that
25 easy. I couldn't even get my hour in at Fun-O-Rama today
26 because of the lines.
27 M.O. ELIMINATOR: This kind of sacrifice has gone too far. What
28 are we to do, Mr. Ortion?
29 ABE: Willis, M.O., we've dealt with problems before — crises and
30 disasters — and I've always had an answer for you. This time
31 is no exception. As you said, Willis, we need fewer people and
32 as you said, M.O., we need something *drastic*. So I have
33 decided, beginning tomorrow, we'll *eliminate all partial people*,
34 *five and under.*
35 WILLIS: Mr. Ortion, you mean kill the *children*?

1   ABE: They're not children. There's no such thing as children.
2   They're partial people!
3   M.O. ELIMINATOR: Mr. Ortion?
4   ABE: What is it, M.O.?
5   M.O. ELIMINATOR: I was just figuring out the statistics, and
6   partial people five and under only make up 4.3 percent of the
7   population. Our research shows that we are overpopulated by
8   eight percent. We've got to do away with more than that.
9   ABE: OK, we'll move it up to seven years.
10 WILLIS: Mr. Ortion, your grandson is only six.
11 ABE: Oh yes, good point. We'll leave it at five.
12 M.O. ELIMINATOR: I have a solution.
13 ABE: Yes, M.O.?
14 M.O. ELIMINATOR: Why don't we also eliminate any partial
15   people who are abnormal, such as the mentally and physically
16   disabled? Those with brain disorders, cripples ...
17 ABE: Excellent idea, but even better, let's go a step further. Let's
18   give all partial people an intelligence test. Only the top twenty
19   percent could remain. We'd not only eliminate more partial
20   people, but think of the race of the future.
21 WILLIS: *(Sighing)* Yeah, more thinkers like you, Abe.
22 ABE: Yeah, this is true. We could even have beauty contests and get
23   rid of the ugly ones.
24 WILLIS: Mr. Ortion, I hate to be the angel's advocate, but isn't
25   this going to cause riots in the colony? I don't think parents
26   will give up their children.
27 ABE: Partial people, not children. Partial people.
28 WILLIS: OK then, partial people. But parents have had five years
29   to grow attached to them. They're not gonna like this. There
30   could be a rebellion.
31 ABE: I suppose you do have a point. Any suggestions?
32 WILLIS: Well, it won't solve the problem as fast, but what if we
33   eliminate partial people that are under nine months? This
34   way the parents won't be as attached.
35 M.O. ELIMINATOR: Good point, Willis. We could also propagate

1   a campaign on how much of a drain from freedom and
2   pleasure it is to have a partial person.

3 ABE: Yes, I think this will work. Let's get this plan in motion.
4   Starting tomorrow, I want you, M.O., to … *(Thunder. Lights*
5   *flicker, like lightning.)*

6 ABE: What is it? Who are you?

7 GOD: *(From Off-stage)* I am the living God.

8 WILLIS: God?

9 M.O. ELIMINATOR: I never considered him.

10 GOD: You know not what you have proposed in your hearts.
11   Should this proposal ever become a reality, the blood of each
12   child's life will be on your heads. You each will be held
13   accountable before me on the Day of Judgment.

14 ABE: But we're not hurting anyone. These aren't people, only
15   partial people.

16 GOD: To me they are my children, and the voice of their blood cries
17   out to me, as did the blood of Abel.

18 ABE: Look, don't point the finger at me. I didn't know. No one told
19   me these partial people are children.

20 WILLIS: I did.

21 ABE: Shut up, Willis!

22 GOD: You greatly err, not knowing the Scriptures. Here, read this!
23   *(Bible may already be on table or may drop down from above.)*

24 M.O. ELIMINATOR: Ooo, look at that book.

25 ABE: Uh, well, I'll look at it later.

26 GOD: Read it!

27 ABE: *(Opens Bible and reads.)* "For you created my inmost being;
28   you knit me together in my mother's womb. My frame was not
29   hidden from you when I was made in secret. When I was
30   woven together in the depths, your eyes saw my unformed
31   body" (Psalm 139:13, 15, 16, author's paraphrase).

32 GOD: I know every person, long before you ever know them. Abe,
33   Willis, M.O., these little ones are people, just like you. To me
34   there's no difference. Willis?

35 WILLIS: Yes, sir?

1 GOD: Read this passage. *(WILLIS takes the Bible.)*
2 WILLIS: Uh-huh. Right away. "The Lord has called me from the
3 womb, from the bowels of my mother has he made mention of
4 my name" (Isaiah 49:1, author's paraphrase). Wow, you knew
5 my name?
6 GOD: Yes. Before the foundation of the world, I knew you and
7 formed you to glorify me. But your present actions are an
8 abomination.
9 M.O. ELIMINATOR: Look, if we aren't to eliminate all the partial
10 peop ... I mean children, what are we supposed to do about
11 our population problem?
12 GOD: You only worry about the masses because of selfishness. You
13 three are afraid you won't get enough. M.O., read this!
14 M.O. ELIMINATOR: "Shall I offer my firstborn for my
15 transgression, the fruit of my body for the sin of my soul? He
16 has shown you what is good and what the Lord requires of
17 you. To act justly and to love mercy and to walk humbly with
18 your God" (Micah 6:7, 8, author's paraphrase).
19 GOD: If you do what I desire you to do, you won't ever worry
20 about yourselves, and I will provide your every need. The
21 choice is yours, but remember, you have been warned! *(ABE,*
22 *WILLIS and M.O. pantomime a discussion during the closing*
23 *narration.)*
24 ANNOUNCER: Three evil beings proposed to do evil, but God
25 intervened. How many times is the evil carried out without
26 questioning the procedure? Remember, if it would have been
27 carried out even one more time, you might not be listening to
28 this now. Till next time. Good night.
29
30
31
32
33
34
35

Blessings or Cursings?

By Dan Rupple

Cast: Announcer, Ben Beeker, Lawrence, Mavis, Hooto Crunk, Clerk, Customer.

Setting: A television game show. The game show takes place at Stage Left, and the record store scenario takes place at Stage Right.

Props: A catalog.

Costumes: Ben wears a suit and tie. All others may be dressed casually. Hooto may wear goofy glasses.

Notes: Crowd noise may be taped.

1   (*LAWRENCE, HOOTO and MAVIS are seated in the audience.*)

2   ANNOUNCER: (*From Off-stage*) **And now it's time for *Blessings or***

3   ***Cursings,* and here is your host, Ben Beeker!** (*BEN enters and*

4   *stands at Stage Left.*)

5   BEN: **Thank you, and welcome once again to *Blessings or Cursings.***

6   **I'm here in our studio audience, and soon I'll be choosing**

7   **today's contestant.** (*To LAWRENCE in audience*) **What about**

8   **you?**

9   LAWRENCE: **Me?**

10   BEN: **Do you know how to play *Blessings or Cursings?***

11   LAWRENCE: **Yes, I do. I watch all the time.**

12   BEN: **Why don't you explain the rules?**

13   LAWRENCE: (*Giggles.*) **I'm so ... nervous.**

14   BEN: **Just relax.**

15   LAWRENCE: **Well, you put me in a situation, then you see how I**

16   **react. If I react properly, I'm blessed, and if I react like a jerk,**

17   **I'm cursed. 'Zat right?**

18   BEN: **Yes, that's right, thank you so much. Now ...**

19   LAWRENCE: **Wait a minute! Don't I get to play?**

20   BEN: **Oh no, I only wanted you to tell our viewers about the rules.**

21   **Thank you!**

22   LAWRENCE: **How uncool! I thought you were gonna pick me.**

23   BEN: **Which only goes to show, you never know how someone is**

24   **going to react.** (*To HOOTO in the audience*) **Now you, sir, what**

25   **is your name?**

26   MAVIS: **He means you, Hooto!**

27   HOOTO: **I know, Mavis. Uh ... my name's Hooto Crunk, and this**

28   **is my wife, Mavis.**

29   BEN: **Nice to meet you, Mavis. Hooto Crunk, and where are you**

30   **from?**

31   HOOTO: **I'm from Woonsocket, Rhode Island.**

32   BEN: **Would you like to play *Blessings or Cursings?***

33   HOOTO: **Come on, who ya fooling? You think I'm here just to**

34   **meet you? I've been in line for two and a half hours. Of course**

35   **I want to play.**

1 BEN: Well then, come on and let's play the game. Now, here's your
2   situation. Hooto, you are a salesclerk in a contemporary
3   record store. Now Hooto, you go over to the scene now, and
4   remember — politeness pays.
5 HOOTO: No sweat!
6 BEN: OK, while Hooto prepares for the scene, let's look in on the
7   buildup to Hooto's situation. *(CLERK enters at Stage Right.*
8   *CUSTOMER enters shortly thereafter.)*
9 CLERK: Hello. May I help you?
10 CUSTOMER: Well, I hope so. I'm looking for an album by Mel
11   Torme.
12 CLERK: Oh, I'm sorry, we don't carry any Mel Torme albums.
13 CUSTOMER: Well, why not? Mel's a fine singer.
14 CLERK: I'm sure he is, but we specialize in contemporary pop
15   rock music.
16 CUSTOMER: Are you calling me old?
17 CLERK: No. I'm just ...
18 CUSTOMER: Well, you're insinuating that you wouldn't carry
19   any albums that I might want because of my age.
20 CLERK: I didn't say *"any* albums" you'd like, just not that
21   particular album.
22 CUSTOMER: Well, why not? You should have something for
23   everyone.
24 CLERK: Well, ma'am, you've got to admit that it'd be kind of
25   stupid to stock every album ever recorded.
26 CUSTOMER: Are you saying that I'm stupid?
27 CLERK: No! By no means.
28 CUSTOMER: First you call me old, now stupid. How dare you
29   insult a customer like that!
30 CLERK: I didn't try to insult you.
31 CUSTOMER: You should thank me for being your customer. It's
32   people like me that pay your bills. And you have the nerve to
33   insult me.
34 CLERK: Look, I'm very sorry. Uh ... perhaps we could order the
35   album.

1   CUSTOMER: How long will that take?

2   CLERK: We'll have it in five to six days.

3   CUSTOMER: OK.

4   CLERK: Fine. Now, which Mel Torme record did you want?

5   CUSTOMER: I want Mel singing "Elvira."

6   CLERK: OK, now let's see … *(Paging through catalog)* oh … I'm

7   sorry, Mel Torme never recorded "Elvira."

8   CUSTOMER: Are you calling me a liar?!

9   CLERK: No, it's just that this catalog covers everything, and it's

10   not in here.

11   CUSTOMER: But you just told me you'd have it in five to six days.

12   CLERK: Well, sure, if it exists, but it doesn't. Torme never sang

13   "Elvira."

14   CUSTOMER: Young man, I personally saw Mel Torme on TV last

15   week singing "Elvira."

16   CLERK: Well, that might be, but he never recorded it.

17   CUSTOMER: Oh, now you change it. You just said he never sang

18   it. Now you say he never recorded it. Young man, you are a

19   lying, insulting militant that buys drugs with the money I

20   spend in your store! *(CLERK exits.)*

21   BEN: OK, let's pause just a moment. Now, Hooto, we're going to

22   let you replace the salesclerk to see your reaction. Let's see if

23   Hooto will retaliate or avoid a major conflict by peaceful

24   toleration. For a blessing or a cursing, Hooto, it's up to you.

25   *(HOOTO crosses over to "record store" at Stage Right.)*

26   CUSTOMER: Young man, are you going to find my record or not?

27   HOOTO: Look lady, where do you come off acting like Attila the

28   Hun? *(Starts pressing her head into the catalog.)* Tell me if you

29   can find it in here. Look real close! Do you see it? I can't hear

30   you!

31   BEN: OK, Hooto, let's stop it right there and see if your reaction

32   would earn you a blessing or a curse. *(HOOTO crosses to game*

33   *show at Stage Left.)*

34   HOOTO: It was a blessing for me just to see her mug stuck in

35   something other than my kisser.

1   BEN: Well, the Word of God says "blessed are the peacemakers"
2   (Matthew 5:9), so your reaction isn't what we're looking for.
3   I'm sorry, Hooto. It looks like you've missed the blessing, and
4   you're going to get a curse.
5   HOOTO: *(Incredulous)* Come on — what? Do I have to have dinner
6   with that lady? What?
7   BEN: Well, Hooto, you'll figure it out. Have a seat, and thank you
8   so much for being our contestant.
9   HOOTO: *(To audience)* See? Nothing happens. You can do
10   whatever you want.
11   BEN: Well, thank you for joining us, and remember — sometimes
12   you can only realize that you are cursed by having others tell
13   you. This is Ben Beeker. Good night from *Blessings or*
14   *Cursings.*
15
16
17
18
19
20
21
22
23
24
25
26
27
28
29
30
31
32
33
34
35

The Blind Seeker

By Dan Rupple

Cast: Cliff (teenage male, and the only speaking part). Nonspeaking roles: Elderly Lady, Three Gang Members, Homeless Man, Teenage Boy, Businessman, Mugger, miscellaneous people on the street.

Setting: A busy city street.

Props: A purse, wallet and "drugs" (pills in a plastic bag).

Costumes: Cliff, Teenage Boy and the people on the street may be dressed casually. Elderly Lady is dressed more formally, befitting her age. The Three Gang Members dress similarly, wearing the same colors and backwards baseball caps. Homeless Man is dressed in torn, holey clothing. Businessman wears a suit. Mugger is dressed all in black.

1 *(CLIFF walks across the stage as if he is walking down a busy city*
2 *street. He is talking out loud to God, oblivious to the actions*
3 *around him.)*
4 **CLIFF: I mean, come on, God, I'm nineteen years old —**
5 **practically ancient — and I don't even have a girlfriend. I**
6 **stand a better chance of being kidnapped by a political**
7 **terrorist than being married anytime in this century.** *(An*
8 *ELDERLY LADY enters and walks behind CLIFF. THREE GANG*
9 *MEMBERS run in and grab her purse and push her down. All of*
10 *the actions are done in a very "cartoony" fashion.)* **You know,**
11 **Lord, I've been asking to serve you, but how am I supposed to**
12 **without a wife? It's like driving on two cylinders. Like driving**
13 **a Yugo in the Daytona 500.** *(A HOMELESS MAN enters and*
14 *begs for food. CLIFF passes right on by.)* **I'm incomplete. I'm**
15 **half a person. I'm like Laurel without Hardy, Astaire without**
16 **Rogers, Milli without Vanilli.** *(A TEENAGE BOY enters and*
17 *walks by. He stops passersby, attempting to sell them drugs.)* **How**
18 **am I supposed to find my calling, my ministry? I know if I had**
19 **a girlfriend, you'd show me where there's a need. You said so**
20 **yourself ... "Where two or more are gathered" ... Come on, I**
21 **need that two!** *(A BUSINESSMAN enters and walks by. A*
22 *MUGGER slugs him in the stomach and steals his wallet. As the*
23 *MUGGER runs away, the BUSINESSMAN is stumbling, hoping*
24 *CLIFF will help him. CLIFF doesn't see him, and the*
25 *BUSINESSMAN collapses on the street. CLIFF stops in his*
26 *tracks.)* **Wait a minute, what am I thinking? It's right in front**
27 **of me. I've been so busy complaining that I've missed it ...**
28 **there was a new girl at church last night. Maybe she's the one ...**
29 **yeah, why didn't I see it before?** *(CLIFF walks Off-stage. The*
30 *VICTIMS of the previous crimes are strewn about the stage.)*
31
32
33
34
35

Celebrity Cornered #2 — Rash Melton

By Dan Rupple

Cast: Wally Wickenshield, Rash Melton.

Setting: The set of a television talk show. Place two chairs at Center Stage, angling inward.

Props: A CD for Wally.

Costumes: A suit and tie for Wally and rock star attire for Rash (torn jeans, black leather, wild hair, etc.).

Sound Effects: Optional theme music.

1　*(Optional theme music plays. WALLY enters and stands at Center*
2　*Stage.)*
3　WALLY:　Hi there! Wally Wickenshield here, with *Celebrity*
4　*Cornered.* My guest today is a true superstar in every sense of
5　the word. He is pop rock music's most successful performer,
6　as well as a hot box office film star. He is currently in town to
7　talk about his concert appearance tomorrow night and the
8　premiere of his new movie that has already caused quite a stir
9　in Hollywood. Please welcome superstar Rash Melton. *(RASH*
10　*enters and he and WALLY sit.)*
11　RASH:　Thank you,Wally. I'm stoked to be here.
12　WALLY:　First off, Rash, we're all looking forward to tomorrow
13　night's concert at the Civic. It is a sellout, isn't it?
14　RASH:　For sure, Wally. As a matter of fact, we've had to add three
15　more shows.
16　WALLY:　That's incredible.
17　RASH:　Not really. Just par for the course. When you're on top,
18　they can't get enough.
19　WALLY:　That seems to be the case. Your new album, *I'm the*
20　*Greatest, You're Crud,* is doing quite well.
21　RASH:　Ya might say everyone's catching the Rash.
22　WALLY:　Yeah, people are itching for you. *(Laughs.)* And now, with
23　a new movie about to premiere, there seems to be Melton-
24　mania like never before.
25　RASH:　Yeah, I'm totally psyched about my new flick.
26　WALLY:　Tell us a little about it.
27　RASH:　Sure. It's called *Mail Order Demon*, and I've got to admit,
28　it's totally scary. Here, scope out this clip. Like it makes
29　*Friday the 13th* look like Palm Sunday. Now, I don't want to
30　give the plot away. That'd be unfair. But let's just say that
31　after you see *Mail Order Demon*, you'll never look at your mail
32　carrier the same way again. You'll totally wig out.
33　WALLY:　Sounds frightening. 'Course it will have to be quite a
34　blockbuster to keep up with your last film.
35　RASH:　You mean *Tract Home Casanova?*

1   WALLY: With Lydia Hearn.
2   RASH: You know, Wally, I don't want to blow the scoop, but let's
3   just say you may be seeing a *Tract Home Casanova Two!*
4   WALLY: Well, this is certainly exciting. You're just keeping so
5   busy.
6   RASH: My buddy upstairs has been totally cool to me.
7   WALLY: Evidently. And I just heard that you've been named *Tiger*
8   *Beat*'s Celebrity of the Year for the second straight year,
9   beating out *Banjo Fever* star Rod Bentley.
10 RASH: For sure. I'm stoked about that, and I really have to thank
11   God. He's the one that made me the great talent I am.
12 WALLY: And I think you can also thank your millions of teenage
13   fans.
14 RASH: To the max. I love those little people. They're so tiny.
15 WALLY: You know, there was a lot of talk that your popularity
16   might be dying after your recent drunk driving arrest. But
17   that doesn't seem to be the case.
18 RASH: Negativo. I think people are willing to forget. It's a
19   testimony that I wasn't killed. The good Lord definitely had
20   his TV tuned on my station that day.
21 WALLY: Rash, you've mentioned God now a couple of times. You
22   aren't trying to make an announcement, are you?
23 RASH: What do you mean?
24 WALLY: Well, you're not going to come out and claim to be a
25   Christian, are you?
26 RASH: Wally, I was born a Christian.
27 WALLY: Rash?!
28 RASH: What's the surprise?
29 WALLY: Well, I just can't picture you … well, it's just not in line
30   with … well, never mind.
31 RASH: Wally, there ain't no way to be as great as I am without
32   God.
33 WALLY: Yes, but usually an artist reflects his values through his
34   work.
35 RASH: Yeah?

1   WALLY: Well, you hardly reflect Christian values. I mean, when I
2   think of love, morality and humility, I don't think of Rash
3   Melton.
4   RASH: Look, Wally, that's what I'm all about. Check out my new
5   album.
6   WALLY: *(Reading song titles off a CD)* "Gag Your Girlfriend with a
7   Spoon," "I Hate Anyone with a Nose," "Sorority Gigolo" ...
8   I'm sorry, Rash.
9   RASH: Wally, those are just the hyper cuts. God wants people to
10   have fun. He's an upbeat kind of God.
11 WALLY: Well ...
12 RASH: Besides, you totally shined on the spiritual tunes.
13 WALLY: Like what?
14 RASH: *(Reading more titles)* Like "I'm God's Gift," "Baby, I'm
15   Heaven," "My Gun Says Your Husband Doesn't Have a
16   Prayer" ... Come on, Wally, we're talking pure gospel.
17 WALLY: You're right, Rash; to me, it's evident exactly where
18   you're coming from. I just hope it's as evident to our viewers.
19   Well, thanks for being here, and good luck with your new
20   movie and your concert.
21 RASH: Wait — you're leaving me on a bummer.
22 WALLY: Till next time, this is Wally Wickenshield with *Celebrity*
23   *Cornered. (Optional theme music plays.)*
24 RASH: What are you saying? You're trying to play mind games
25   with me. You're not going to get away with it. My head is
26   totally sealed.
27
28
29
30
31
32
33
34
35

Commencement Address

By Dan Rupple (with a thank you to Bob Bennett)

Cast: Speaker.

Setting: A college graduation ceremony. A podium is at Center Stage.

Props: None.

Costumes: Commencement robe and mortarboard.

1   *(SPEAKER enters and stands at a podium.)*
2   SPEAKER: Thank you, Dean Witter ... Students, faculty, alumni,
3   parents, in-laws, outlaws, military recruiters, IRS agents,
4   Amway salesmen, Bert and Ernie, Burt and Loni, Siskel and
5   Ebert, and all the rest ...
6   I'm honored that you've chosen me to deliver the 1992
7   commencement speech here in the lovely surroundings of the
8   campus of the University of Texas at Do-Wack-A-Do. Indeed,
9   this very spot which we occupy today is rife with meaningful
10   history. Just a few short decades ago, there was a Jim and
11   Tammy Kung-Fu theatre here ... My, how times change.
12   Despite the fact that often "all a youngster wants out of
13   school is himself," here at Do-Wack-A-Do-U, you've received
14   something so valuable — more than the wedgies from those
15   dinky desks. You've received an education and a square hat
16   with a tassel. Who designed these, anyway?
17   However, this is not an ending, but a beginning ... the
18   beginning of a new paragraph, the beginning of a beautiful
19   friendship, the beginning of today. You know today. Today is
20   the beginning of the rest of your life, today is the tomorrow
21   you worried about yesterday ... and ... *Today* is Al Roker's
22   meal ticket.
23   As you began in the fall ... outlasted the winter ... the
24   renewal of spring, remember your schooling didn't last as
25   long as *Gilligan's Island,* and they only set out on a three-hour
26   tour ... a three-hour tour. Why did the Howells take all that
27   luggage? I don't know about that, but I do know that "truth
28   is a bird precariously perched on the narrow gate of life,
29   dropping truth bombs upon those who are looking upward
30   with open minds."
31   But even these thoughts pale in comparison to the heed of
32   the old proverb, "He who fails at duck hunting isn't throwing
33   the dog high enough."
34   I think Jed Clampett summed it up best when he said,
35   "Always remember that even Abraham Lincoln had great

1 difficulty getting an education, but what can you expect from
2 a guy who couldn't play football or basketball?"

3 In a world where dropouts either drive Porsches or go to
4 night court, we in the middle must transcend our middleness.
5 We must stand up, rise up, rear back, get down, bear down,
6 buck up, hunker down, get back to the basics and "Get back,
7 Jojo, to where we once belonged."

8 We must remain firmly rooted with our feet on the solid
9 ground and our hearts opened to heaven ... and yet what of
10 space? You know, space ... the final frontier, the thing you
11 never have enough of in import automobiles, but too much of
12 between your teeth after eating pork.

13 As you are seated here today with your classmates, look at
14 the person on your right ... and now at the person on your
15 left. Did you feel any grating sensation in your neck? Any
16 diminishing of your normal range of movement? Have you
17 thought about a chiropractor? Have you looked in the Yellow
18 Pages under "K"?

19 In closing, I encourage you to hold in highest disregard
20 what I have told you here. Keep it always hidden in the very
21 bottom of the dresser drawer of your heart.

22 I wish you every success as you graduate today. The
23 journey of a thousand miles begins with one small step for
24 man and a giant leap for a guy with really short legs.

25 Hail, hail, you groovy dudes and dudettes. I'll be behind
26 you every step of the way. Have a twitchin' summer. Stay just
27 the way you are. Don't ever change. God bless you and
28 remember ... the fear of the Lord is the beginning of wisdom ...
29 and the fear of that stupid pink bunny with the drum
30 marching through your house late at night will drive you
31 crazy.
32
33
34
35

Ed Herman's Talk Radio — Ed Knows

By Dan Rupple

Cast: Ed Herman, Caller #1 (female), Caller #2 (female), Caller #3 (male), Caller #4 (male), Caller #5 (female).

Setting: A talk radio studio. Place a table and chair at Center Stage.

Props: Headphones and a push-button telephone.

Costumes: Casual attire.

Sound Effects: Drowning and gurgling sounds, optional theme music.

Note: The callers are Off-stage, speaking into a microphone.

1   ED: OK, it's about a quarter past the hour on Ed Herman's talk
2   radio show. I'm Ed Herman. Give me a call. You got a difficult
3   problem and you need a solution? Call me, Ed Herman. I
4   know. Maybe you're in a situation that has you totally
5   perplexed. Give me a call. Just dial Ed Herman. This is the
6   place to get the answers. OK, line one is flashing. Hello, you're
7   on the Ed Herman show.

8   CALLER #1: Ed? This is Bernadette.

9   ED: Hi, Bernadette. What's your problem?

10   CALLER #1: I kind of have an emergency. I'm in my basement,
11   and one of our water pipes broke. I'm talking total flood, Ed.
12   What can I do?

13   ED: Gee, sounds like quite a mess.

14   CALLER #1: Yeah, right now I'm standing on my washing
15   machine, and the water's already up to my knees.

16   ED: Kind of like a built-in splasher pool, huh?

17   CALLER #1: What?

18   ED: Nothing. Just a little joke.

19   CALLER #1: I remember my husband said that if this ever
20   happened I was supposed to shut off the main valve, but I
21   don't know where it is. Do you?

22   ED: I knew you were going to ask me that.

23   CALLER #1: What do I do, Ed? The water's getting pretty high!

24   ED: Tell you what — give me some time to think about it. Why
25   don't you call in tomorrow?

26   CALLER #1: Ed, you're supposed to have all the answers. I need
27   help now. There's got to be something I can do!

28   ED: You're right — seems like there would be something you could
29   do, but gee … So let's move on. Thanks for calling.

30   CALLER #1: *(Amidst drowning and gurgling sounds)* What? Ed,
31   help! Don't hang up! *(ED hangs up.)*

32   ED: You're listening to Ed Herman's radio talk show, where the
33   answers are the issues. There are still some lines open. Just
34   dial ED KNOWS. Line two, hello. You're on with Ed Herman.

35   CALLER #2: Hi, Ed. This is Margaret. I'm a little nervous. My

1   question is kind of personal.

2   ED: Don't worry, we're all informed people here.

3   CALLER #2: Well, I have a fifteen-year-old daughter, and I wanted

4   to know what I should do concerning birth control.

5   ED: Well, it's a little late for that.

6   CALLER #2: Huh?

7   ED: Being that you had her fifteen years ago.

8   CALLER #2: No, Ed, not for me, for my daughter.

9   ED: Oh, I see. Well, that *is* a problem. I mean, you don't want any

10   unwanted pregnancies, but if you help her, she might think

11   you're encouraging her. Am I right?

12   CALLER #2: Exactly. Oh, Ed, you have so much insight. I don't

13   want to be supportive of something she shouldn't even be

14   involved in.

15   ED: Right, so I think it should really be between your daughter and

16   her husband.

17   CALLER #2: Her husband? Ed, she's not married!

18   ED: Oh. Well, that's a whole other story. Thanks for calling. *(ED*

19   *hangs up.)* You're listening to Ed Herman's show. The man

20   with the answers to all problems, no matter how difficult they

21   seem to you. Before I go to line three, a reminder on

22   tomorrow's show. My topic deals with defense. The question:

23   How do we limit the arms race without leaving our country

24   defenseless? And you can be sure that I'll have some

25   innovative answers. But let me clue you in — I don't think

26   anyone should have more than two arms, and I don't care

27   what country they're from. So tune in tomorrow. Is that

28   tomorrow? Well, just tune in and find out. Let's go to line

29   three. Hello, you're on with Ed Herman.

30   CALLER #3: Hey, Ed, this is Barney. Got a question for you.

31   ED: Fire away.

32   CALLER #3: Who's buried in Grant's tomb?

33   ED: Listen, Barney, I don't know if you listen to my show, but I'm

34   not one to banter back and forth about philosophical issues.

35   CALLER #3: No. It's just a joke.

1   ED: A joke? Not to Grant or to whoever is in there. *(Hangs up.)*
2   Let's go on to line four.
3   CALLER #4: Yeah, Ed, I just got laid off, and I don't know what
4   to do. I'm pretty down.
5   ED: That is a problem. I mean, with the way unemployment is, I
6   wouldn't be surprised if you don't find another job.
7   CALLER #4: Yeah, and I'm married and I have four children.
8   ED: And no job?! With a wife and kids?!
9   CALLER #4: That's why I'm calling. What should I do? My house
10   payment's due next week.
11   ED: You own a house?
12   CALLER #4: Yeah.
13   ED: Well, you'll probably lose that, don'tcha think?
14   CALLER #4: It's hopeless, Ed. Maybe I should kill myself.
15   ED: Wait — don't be so hasty. Do you have life insurance?
16   CALLER #4: Yeah, two hundred thousand dollars worth.
17   ED: Well, you're covered there. That's sure to take care of your
18   family and the house.
19   CALLER #4: I've got some pills here, Ed.
20   ED: Yeah, that'd probably work, wouldn't it?
21   CALLER #4: Darn right it would. You've convinced me.
22   ED: Well, good.
23   CALLER #4: Aw, gee, these stupid caps. How do you get these tops
24   off?
25   ED: Yeah, those caps are crazy. I never did figure those out.
26   CALLER #4: I'll shoot it off!
27   ED: Well, I hope I helped you. Be sure to call back, I'm dying to
28   hear how it all worked out. Well, not dying in the sense that
29   you ... *(Hangs up.)* Well, just like that caller, we're almost out
30   of time. One more call. Let's go to line five.
31   CALLER #5: Yes, is this Ed Herman?
32   ED: You got it, lady.
33   CALLER #5: Yeah, this is the first time I've listened to your
34   program, and I've been amazed.
35   ED: Well, thank you.

1   CALLER #5: No — I mean you don't know anything.
2   ED: I don't?
3   CALLER #5: You haven't answered one question.
4   ED: I had to?
5   CALLER #5: And another thing — who made you an authority,
6   anyway?
7   ED: I don't know.
8   CALLER #5: You're a rip-off, Herman. Those callers are hurting,
9   they need answers, and ...
10 ED: Hold it right there. I do know one thing.
11 CALLER #5: What?
12 ED: *(Puzzled look, then optional theme plays.)* That's our theme
13   music. Thanks for joining us. Be with us tomorrow for Ed
14   Herman's talk radio show. When life's questions get too
15   complicated for you, turn to this man, Ed Herman. I know.
16   I've got the answers you're looking for. Until tomorrow,
17   remember — Ed knows. He really does.
18
19
20
21
22
23
24
25
26
27
28
29
30
31
32
33
34
35

Enroad Brickman

By Dan Rupple

Cast: Enroad Brickman, J.C., Mr. D.

Setting: Heaven. If you have a fog machine, use it to make clouds. Later, when Mr. D. enters, aim a red spot on the clouds if you have access to theatrical lighting. (A spotlight and a red gel may also be rented.)

Props: None.

Costumes: Enroad Brickman is dressed ultra-hip, but his clothes are torn from an accident. Mr. D. wears all-black or all-red clothing.

1   *(ENROAD BRICKMAN walks in. He is in his early twenties,*
2   *dressed ultra-hip, but his clothes are torn from an accident. He*
3   *speaks to an unseen voice.)*
4 **J.C.:** *(From Off-stage)* **Can I help you?**
5 **ENROAD: Yeah, is this heaven?**
6 **J.C.: Yes, it is.**
7 **ENROAD: Awesome! The name's Brickman, Enroad Brickman.**
8 **J.C.: I'm sorry, you're not on the list.**
9 **ENROAD: Get out! You can't have a party without Enroad**
10   **Brickman. Maybe you don't know what kind of guy I am.**
11 **J.C.: I know exactly what kind of guy you are.**
12 **ENROAD: Cool! Yeah, I'm the guy who drank two kegs of beer at**
13   **Marsha Waynewright's party last month. Two kegs! Through**
14   **my nose! That alone gets me into more places than American**
15   **Express.**
16 **J.C.: I'm sorry, Enroad. That doesn't make it.**
17 **ENROAD: All right, let's be real. I know that a dude like you and**
18   **a dude like me really don't go together. I mean, I'm no angel.**
19   **I've messed up a few times. Like the time I freaked out in Mr.**
20   **Hansen's waterbed store with that ice pick. But I was gonna**
21   **pay him back.**
22 **J.C.: No, Enroad, there still isn't a place for you.**
23 **ENROAD: No place?! Look, I'm not ready for this.**
24 **J.C.: That's your problem, Enroad. You aren't ready.**
25 **ENROAD: And you would be? I mean, do you know what kind of**
26   **day I've had? Like I'm hangin' out with my buddies and we**
27   **run out of booze; so, like a jerk, I volunteer to drive to Narby's**
28   **Liquor. Mega-mistake, you know. And there I am, swerving to**
29   **Motley Crue, when this semi truck decides to plow right**
30   **across my steering wheel. Like, thanks for the notice!**
31 **J.C.: Everyone must be ready to face God at any moment. No one**
32   **is guaranteed tomorrow.**
33 **ENROAD: Look, I was a busy guy. I didn't have time for all that**
34   **stuff about God.**
35 **J.C.: Now it's cost you everything for all eternity.**

1   ENROAD: Oh, I get it. You want some payola. Let's see ... I could
2   hock my board, and I got a good set of fins.
3   J.C.: I paid the price of sin so that you could be redeemed and enter
4   into eternal life. If only you had accepted it.
5   ENROAD: Say what? Who are you?
6   J.C.: I'm Jesus Christ.
7   ENROAD: Jump back! You're supposed to be dead. I mean, isn't
8   that what Easter's for? ... Look, somebody on the radio told
9   me there was a rock 'n' roll heaven. You're in luck. I play
10   drums.
11   J.C.: I am the only way!
12   ENROAD: Come on. How many times have I heard that kind of
13   junk before?
14   J.C.: But you never believed it.
15   ENROAD: Hey, man, what am I supposed to do now? I mean, I
16   come all the way up here expecting a rad party, and I'm not
17   on the list ... *(Clouds turn to dark red smoke. Enter MR. D.)*
18   MR. D.: Mr. Brickman?
19   ENROAD: Yeah? *(Seeing him)* Whoa! Weren't you in that movie
20   *Night of the Living Dead?*
21   MR. D.: I have a place for you over here. *(MR. D. exits.)*
22   ENROAD: All right. Good, dude. A voice I recognize ... *(Exiting)* Is
23   it just me, or is it getting hot in here?
24
25
26
27
28
29
30
31
32
33
34
35

Equal Time

By Dan Rupple

Cast: Hawkings, Kirkwood, Edgar.

Setting: An office. Place a desk at Center Stage.

Props: A telephone.

Costumes: Kirkwood is dressed for racquetball. Edgar is in a business suit.

1   *(KIRKWOOD sits atop his desk. EDGAR enters.)*
2   **KIRKWOOD:** OK, Edgar. You said it was urgent. Let's get on with
3   it. I got a racquetball game at 11:30.
4   **EDGAR:** Well, Mr. Kirkwood, I know you're a busy man, being
5   head of network programming and all; and if I could've dealt
6   with this at a lower level, I would have, sir, but ...
7   **KIRKWOOD:** Edgar, get to the point.
8   **EDGAR:** Well, sir, last night, after the news, we broadcast an
9   editorial reply saying that God was dead.
10   **KIRKWOOD:** Sure, it was on right before our big *Call Girl for*
11   *President* miniseries.
12   **EDGAR:** Yes sir, and what a hit that miniseries is going to be.
13   **KIRKWOOD:** I'm quite proud of that one. It was my niece's idea.
14   She'll be twelve next month.
15   **EDGAR:** I've always said creativity knows no age limits. But
16   getting back to the editorial, well, now he wants equal time.
17   **KIRKWOOD:** Who?
18   **EDGAR:** God, sir.
19   **KIRKWOOD:** God?
20   **EDGAR:** Yes, sir.
21   **KIRKWOOD:** But he's dead!
22   **EDGAR:** Not according to him, sir.
23   **KIRKWOOD:** *(Pushing intercom button on telephone)* Angie, get
24   Hawkings in here and put my court reservation on hold. *(To*
25   *EDGAR)* Since when did God care about TV? Doesn't he
26   usually talk through burning bushes or something?
27   **EDGAR:** That's old hat, sir. Besides, the networks do a lot better
28   in the ratings than your average shrub.
29   **KIRKWOOD:** That's luck for us too, Edgar, because I know as
30   much about planting trees as Regis Philbin.
31   **EDGAR:** That's very funny, sir.
32   **KIRKWOOD:** Make a note of that. Maybe we can use it on one of
33   those Andy Rooney things or something. *(Enter HAWKINGS.)*
34   **HAWKINGS:** You wanted to see me, sir?
35   **KIRKWOOD:** Yes, Hawkings, we've got a problem. Our network

1   has had a demand for equal time from *God!*
2   HAWKINGS: But he's dead, sir. I heard it on our news last night.
3   EDGAR: I guess we were wrong, Mr. Hawkings.
4   HAWKINGS: Well, what exactly does he want?
5   EDGAR: I think he just wants equal time to let people know that
6   he's around.
7   KIRKWOOD: Any ideas, Hawkings?
8   HAWKINGS: Well, we could just let him do tomorrow's editorial
9   rebuttal.
10   KIRKWOOD: You mean just let him spout off in front of a live
11   camera? Nothing doing. Besides, tomorrow's editorial is right
12   between that skimpy swimsuit special and part two of our
13   miniseries. Putting God in the middle would quench the whole
14   spirit of the evening.
15   HAWKINGS: We could put him on one of our interview shows.
16   KIRKWOOD: Oh, that's cruel! Putting God, someone with
17   absolutely no journalistic experience, up to the scrutiny of the
18   likes of Bryant Gumbel or Geraldo Rivera. No, I wanna play
19   fair. You never know when down the road you're gonna need
20   God on your side, am I right? No, we need something fair, but
21   where we can have total control of him.
22   HAWKINGS: I got it! How about an Easter special?
23   EDGAR: In October?
24   KIRKWOOD: Yeah, no one will watch it. That will really bury this
25   thing.
26   EDGAR: That won't work, sir.
27   KIRKWOOD: What?
28   EDGAR: Burying God. It's been tried. Uh, that's kind of how
29   Easter came about.
30   HAWKINGS: What a time for this to happen. First cable, then
31   God!
32   EDGAR: And right before ratings month.
33   KIRKWOOD: That's it!
34   EDGAR: What is, sir?
35   KIRKWOOD: We're looking at this all wrong. Let's put him on a

1   series. It could do miracles for the ratings.
2   EDGAR: I don't know about miracles. He only wanted to talk. He
3   might charge extra.
4   KIRKWOOD: Yeah, think of it. He could heal people on *Chicago*
5   *Hope.*
6   HAWKINGS: Or how about *Cheers*? He could change water into
7   wine.
8   KIRKWOOD: No, no, I've got it. He could walk out to *The Love*
9   *Boat.* Get ahold of his agent and set this up.
10 EDGAR: His agent?
11 KIRKWOOD: Yeah, everyone has an agent. The ten percent has to
12   go somewhere. 'Course God's agent probably takes ninety
13   percent.
14 EDGAR: Ninety percent, Mr. Kirkwood?
15 KIRKWOOD: Everyone knows you only give ten percent to God.
16   Oh, that's funny. I hope you're writing these down.
17 HAWKINGS: Wait a minute, we can avoid this whole thing.
18 KIRKWOOD: How's that, Hawkings?
19 HAWKINGS: Two weeks ago, I recall someone saying "God bless
20   you" at the end of *Hee Haw.*
21 KIRKWOOD: That's equal time if ever I've heard it. Good work,
22   Hawkings.
23 HAWKINGS: *(Exiting)* Thank you, sir.
24 KIRKWOOD: You know, Edgar, it does a heart proud to be able to
25   do what's right and to be fair to all concerned. And only in
26   America. Yes, America, one nation, under ... uh, so Edgar,
27   you ever play racquetball? *(Both exit.)*
28
29
30
31
32
33
34
35

Fadscene — Disco vs. Hippie

By Dan Rupple

Cast: Theda Williams, Flash Bronze, Zack Freppo.

Setting: The *Fadscene* television set. There are three chairs at Center Stage — Theda's in the middle, Flash is to her right, and Zack is to her left. The guests' chairs may be angled in slightly.

Props: None.

Costumes: Theda should wear a suit. Flash should wear a white suit *a la* John Travolta in *Saturday Night Fever,* with a carnation boutonniere. Zack should be dressed hippie style: bell-bottom jeans, a headband, a long-haired wig, tie-dyed T-shirt, etc.

Sound Effects: Optional theme music.

1   (*THEDA sits at Center Stage. FLASH sits at THEDA's right and*
2   *ZACK sits at her left. Optional theme music plays.*)
3   THEDA: Good evening, and welcome to *Fadscene*. I'm your
4   *Fadscene* moderator, Theda Williams. If you've watched
5   *Fadscene* before, you know that we discuss and debate fads —
6   past, present and future — that influence our lifestyles. On
7   *Fadscene* today, we will be discussing two fads of the past:
8   first, the hippie movement, a fad from the late sixties and early
9   seventies; and second, the disco craze, a scene prevalent in the
10   late seventies. My guests are: to my right, representing the
11   hippie movement, Zack Freppo, a former hippie leader on
12   West Coast campuses who now owns a health food store in
13   Santa Monica, California; and to my left, Flash Bronze, the
14   former owner of Flash's Discotheque in New Jersey, who is
15   presently unemployed. Gentlemen, I welcome you to *Fadscene*.
16   ZACK and FLASH: Thank you, pleasure, (*etc.*)
17   THEDA: Zack, I'll start with you. The hippie movement was a
18   culture best exemplified by rock festivals, drugs, love-ins, long
19   hair and terms like "groovy," "cool" and "out-of-sight." How
20   has the hippie movement affected our society through the
21   years?
22   ZACK: Well, man, you know, Thelma ...
23   THEDA: *Theda!*
24   ZACK: Yeah, that's cool, whatever you relate to. I just think the
25   impact of the hippie movement is so obvious. We were a peace
26   army that challenged every value in existence. Nothing like
27   that disco garbage. That, man, was just a flash in the pan.
28   That's why you call it a craze.
29   THEDA: OK, Flash, Zack does have a point. Disco seems to have
30   left as fast as it came. What are your thoughts on this
31   phenomenon?
32   FLASH: First off, Ms. Williams, disco is not dead. We might be
33   sitting a song out, but we'll be back boogying — the fever is
34   still high. And secondarily, Mr. Freppo implied that we haven't
35   had any effect on culture. Well, if you recall, the hippies wore

1	filthy patched-up jeans and tie-dyed shirts, but we added
2	elegance and respectability to today's youth, with designer
3	jeans, silk shirts, and baggy suits and slacks.
4	ZACK: Slow it down, man. We dressed up, too. I personally had two
5	Nehru jackets, man.
6	FLASH: Big deal. What a rip-off! You guys stole that idea from the
7	clothes worn in India.
8	ZACK: Hey, man, look who's talking about stealing. What about
9	those necklaces and chains you wear? Me and my old lady
10	wore love beads and medallions before you could bump.
11	THEDA: Gentlemen, one primary aspect of both the hippie and
12	disco fads was music. Your philosophies and lifestyles both
13	emerged in music and later in films such as *Easy Rider* and
14	*Saturday Night Fever.*
15	ZACK: Oh man, not fair. How can you say those two flicks in the
16	same breath? I mean, Dennis Hopper could break Travolta's
17	legs any day of the week.
18	FLASH: Typical, you would get into violence. Where's all your
19	peace talk now, Freppo?
20	ZACK: Oh, yeah? Well, at least we weren't sissies. While you were
21	taking dancing lessons, we were throwing rocks in the streets
22	of Chicago.
23	FLASH: Dancers are in better shape than some athletes. Travolta
24	doesn't need a motorcycle to get around. Hopper couldn't
25	boogie down for ten minutes.
26	ZACK: Hey, man, don't get on my man Hopper's trip. That cat's
27	hip. I still think he was an eggman.
28	THEDA: An eggman?
29	ZACK: Yeah, it's from the *Magical Mystery Tour* album. It says,
30	"They are the eggmen." Wow, that was groovy.
31	FLASH: Well, if they were the eggmen, who are you?
32	ZACK: Man, you are a spacer. "I am the walrus." *(FLASH laughs.)*
33	Hey, who are you laughing at? At least we didn't listen to
34	pumped-up elevator music. Hendrix and Janis Joplin could
35	wipe out anyone you got.

1 THEDA: I'd like to ask you about …
2 FLASH: Look, Freppo, the Bee Gees sold more records than all of
3   yours put together.
4 ZACK: Those traitors! They started on our side. I knew them
5   before they sang like girls.
6 FLASH: Well, at least they're stayin' alive!
7 THEDA: OK, gentlemen. Let us move on. Obviously you two are
8   miles apart.
9 FLASH: I wish we were farther apart. His smell is wilting my
10   carnation.
11 ZACK: These disco ducks, they can't groove in the real world. Take
12   them outside of four walls and a flashy floor, and they aren't
13   human.
14 THEDA: Now Flash, Zack does have a point. The hippie movement
15   manifested itself in all areas of life, but disco does center
16   around one activity.
17 FLASH: Oh, how shallow can you be? Disco is a lifestyle, a
18   philosophy. It's expression in its most mature form.
19 THEDA: Well, how do you express it out on the streets, away from
20   the disco?
21 FLASH: Well, we have roller disco!
22 THEDA: You mean on roller skates?
23 FLASH: It's pure art.
24 ZACK: I don't believe it. You never saw Abbie Hoffman on skates.
25 FLASH: Well, of course. How could you know anything about
26   ground travel? All of your trips are way out in the ozone.
27 THEDA: Gentlemen, I'm going to have to stop you there — we're
28   out of time. Well, once again we've investigated two fads that
29   dictated personal lifestyles, and we see those values changed
30   with the times. But one thing is certain, if we are going to set
31   values for our lives, it's best to set them on something that
32   never changes. You don't want your life to be out of style
33   before you're out of life. This is Theda Williams, inviting you
34   to join us next time on *Fadscene*, when our topic will be "Punk
35   versus Preppie." Good night. *(Optional theme music plays.)*

Faith on Trial

By Dan Rupple

Cast: Announcer, Judge, Court Clerk, Larry Luckbill, Elmo Casey, Bernie Whallings, Evelyn Mudley, Mrs. Raul Jurgenson, Johnny, Jury (six jurors if possible).

Setting: A televised courtroom. Place a desk at Upstage Center for the Judge. At the Judge's left is a podium for the witness stand. Place two chairs at Stage Right for Larry Luckbill and Elmo Casey, and two at Stage Left for Mrs. Raul Jurgenson and Bernie Whallings. Chairs should be set up at Stage Left (side to audience) for the jury.

Props: Gavel, Bible.

Costumes: A robe for the Judge and business attire for the others.

1   *(The JUDGE sits at his desk. The COURT CLERK stands by the*
2   *witness stand. ELMO and LARRY sit on the chairs at Stage Right.*
3   *MRS. RAUL JURGENSON and BERNIE WHALLINGS sit on the*
4   *chairs at Stage Left. The JURY sits on chairs [side to audience]*
5   *at Stage Left. All freeze as ANNOUNCER speaks.)*
6   ANNOUNCER: *(From Off-stage)* **Welcome once again to *Faith on***
7   ***Trial*, the show where we take the camera into the land's most**
8   **important scene of judgment and truth. Today's case involves**
9   **the plaintiff, Mrs. Raul Jurgenson, whose home was broken**
10   **into and robbed of thousands of dollars in cash and personal**
11   **property. Mrs. Jurgenson is represented by former game**
12   **show host Bernie Whallings. And this is the accused, our**
13   **defendant, Mr. Larry Luckbill. Mr. Luckbill is represented by**
14   **attorney Elmo Casey. The session is about to resume. Let's**
15   **join them now.**
16   JUDGE: *(Pounds gavel.)* **OK, let's have a little order in the court.**
17   **Now, I think everyone's back from lunch, so before it begins**
18   **attacking my stomach, let's continue the questioning and**
19   **wrap this case up. Mr. Casey?** *(ELMO is asleep.)* **Mr. Casey?**
20   LARRY: *(To ELMO)* **Wake up!**
21   ELMO: **Huh? Oh! Your Honor, before we break for lunch, my**
22   **client would like to have a brief word with you.**
23   JUDGE: **Very well.**
24   LARRY: *(Standing)* **Your Honor, I don't think I'm getting a fair**
25   **trial. I can't believe what's going on here. It's a circus.**
26   JUDGE: **What are you saying?**
27   LARRY: **Your Honor, none of the evidence even remotely points to**
28   **me, but everyone here refuses to believe I'm innocent. I've**
29   **even proven that I was nowhere near that house, but the jury**
30   **has obviously already made their decision.** *(JURY makes*
31   *noises, slugging fist, etc.)* **And my lawyer won't even defend**
32   **me. He's slept through the whole trial!**
33   JUDGE: **Don't worry, Larry, you're not going to be convicted.**
34   LARRY: *(Unconvinced)* **Sure …**
35   JUDGE: **Larry, I know you're innocent.**

1   LARRY: Yeah, but the jury!

2   JUDGE: Look, I'm the judge, and no matter what's said, I know

3   the truth. Just trust me. Have a little faith.

4   LARRY: Well ...

5   JUDGE: Take your seat. *(LARRY sits.)* OK, let the trial continue.

6   BERNIE: *(Stands.)* Your Honor, I'd like to call, from the beautiful

7   city of Pineville, Miss Evelyn Mudley to the stand. Evelyn,

8   come on down. *(Runs down excited like in game show. The*

9   *COURT CLERK swears her in.)* What is your name and where

10   do you live?

11   EVELYN: My name is Evelyn Mudley, and I live across the street

12   from Mrs. Raul Jurgenson.

13   BERNIE: Do you have anyone with you here today?

14   EVELYN: Yes, my best friend Helen, my cousin Mike, and my

15   sister-in-law Mavis.

16   BERNIE: Well, that's great. Good to have you here. Well, Evelyn,

17   you know how the trial works, so sit back, relax and let's start

18   with the first question.

19   JUDGE: Bernie, get on with it! Your game show days are over.

20   BERNIE: Your Honor, a lot of producers watch this show. You

21   never know. Evelyn, where were you the night of the crime in

22   question?

23   EVELYN: I was in my house watching television by my front

24   window.

25   BERNIE: That's correct for five points, Evelyn. Did you see a man

26   break in at the Jurgensons' house?

27   EVELYN: Yes I did, about 10:30, right after one of those news

28   briefs with Barbara Walters.

29   BERNIE: By the way, Barbara will be hosting a special Monday

30   night at 9:30 Eastern Standard Time. Her guests will be

31   Robert DeNiro and Julia Roberts. Don't miss it!

32   JUDGE: Bernie?!

33   BERNIE: Evelyn, could you describe the man you saw?

34   EVELYN: Yes, he was short.

35   BERNIE: Say what, about five foot three?

1 EVELYN: Oh, no, I mean short! This was a midget. I'd say four
2 foot two at best. He had blonde hair, a full beard, glasses and
3 a huge nose.
4 LARRY: Finally! The truth!
5 BERNIE: Now Evelyn, is this man that you saw robbing the
6 Jurgenson house in this courtroom today?
7 EVELYN: Yes he is, Mr. Whallings. That's him right there. *(Points*
8 *to LARRY.)*
9 LARRY: I don't believe it!
10 BERNIE: Now when Mr. Luckbill left the house, he was carrying
11 some things. And for five points, Evelyn, what was he
12 carrying?
13 EVELYN: Well, it's quite a list.
14 BERNIE: I know it is, Evelyn, and to help you out, Johnny Merrill
15 will read your list for you. Johnny?
16 JOHNNY: *(From Off-stage)* Thank you, Bernie. Yes, the thief was
17 carrying a Zenith black-and-white portable television; a new
18 early American sofa, love seat and chair; a Maytag full-cycle
19 washer and top-loading dryer; and a full set of the new, fully
20 illustrated World Book encyclopedia. World Book, designed
21 with your mind in mind. And that's not all — a valuable
22 collection of jewelry, two hundred dollars in cash and a new
23 microwave oven!
24 BERNIE: Thank you, Johnny! And Evelyn, he carried all of that
25 stuff by himself?
26 EVELYN: Yes, and in one trip.
27 LARRY: Your Honor, that's impossible.
28 JUDGE: Let me be the judge. Just relax, Larry.
29 BERNIE: OK, Evelyn, for fifty-five bonus points, how much would
30 you say all of that merchandise is worth?
31 EVELYN: Uh, gee, this is hard. I'll say ... seven thousand, eight
32 hundred, fifty-nine dollars and fifty-three cents.
33 BERNIE: OK, Evelyn says seven thousand, eight hundred, fifty-
34 nine dollars and fifty-three cents, and the actual amount
35 stolen was ... seven thousand, eight hundred, fifty-nine

1   dollars and fifty-three cents! Evelyn, you are our winner!

2   EVELYN: Oh, I can't believe it. This is fantastic!

3   JUDGE: Bernie, come on.

4   BERNIE: Yes, Your Honor. Congratulations, Evelyn. Your Honor,

5   members of the jury, that's my case for today. Thanks for

6   watching.

7   JUDGE: OK, we've heard all of the evidence. Now does the jury

8   have a verdict?

9   JUROR: Yes, we do, Your Honor. The man is a maniac. I don't

10   want him in my neighborhood. We say guilty! Lock him up in

11   a piranha tank.

12   LARRY: I demand a new trial!

13   JUROR: Shut up, you maniac. You ever come around my house,

14   I'll …

15   JUDGE: *(Pounds gavel.)* Order! Now, I've been sitting here all day

16   listening to accusations, personal prejudices and hatred, and

17   unfortunately, an out-of-place game show. But what I haven't

18   heard is the truth, which ultimately all judgments must be

19   based on. So with that in mind, I find the defendant innocent

20   of all charges. Larry, you're free to go. Case dismissed.

21   *(Pounds gavel. All freeze.)*

22   ANNOUNCER: Well, there you have it. A last-minute turn of

23   events. And I believe we've seen that no matter how you may

24   be unfairly accused, no matter how bad circumstances around

25   you seem, no matter how few come to your defense, you must

26   always trust the outcome to the one that judges fair and true.

27   Thank you for joining us, and we'll see you on our next

28   installment of *Faith on Trial.*

29

30

31

32

33

34

35

The Funnymooners

By Dave Toole

Cast: Ned Morton, Raff Kampden.

Setting: Ned Morton's apartment.

Props: A piece of thin cardboard to resemble a lottery ticket, and a telephone.

Costumes: A coonskin cap ("Raccoon Lodge hat"), T-shirt, vest and jeans for Ned. Raff may wear a dark-colored suit and tie — something out of the fifties, if possible — and maybe some extra waist padding. He wears a coonskin hat as well.

1   *(NED comes running in wearing a Raccoon Lodge hat. He is in a*
2   *hurry and slams the door behind himself.)*
3   **RAFF:** *(Off-stage)* **C'mon, Morton, open this door!**
4   **NED: Not a chance, Raff. Not till you calm down out there.**
5   **RAFF: Listen, Morton, you let me in right now, or I'm goin'**
6   **downstairs to get the key from the landlord.**
7   **NED: No, you won't, 'cause Tricky already lost his key last week.**
8   **Hee-hee.**
9   **RAFF: All right, that does it. Morton, you let me in right now!**
10   **NED: OK, Raff, but first you got to promise not to hit me.** *(Pause)*
11   **Raff?**
12   **RAFF: All right, all right, just let me in.**
13   **NED: You promise not to hit me?**
14   **RAFF: Yeah, I promise.**
15   **NED: Cross your heart and hope to die?**
16   **RAFF: Yeah, yeah, cross my heart and hope to die.**
17   **NED: Stick a needle in your eye?**
18   **RAFF: Would you just open this door?**
19   **NED: All right, all right.** *(NED opens the door and RAFF enters with*
20   *his raccoon hat on.)*
21   **RAFF: What'd you lock me out like that for?**
22   **NED: What'd you chase me all the way home like that for? I ain't**
23   **never seen you so mad before.**
24   **RAFF: That's because I've never been stabbed in the back like that**
25   **before. And by my best friend! Make that my *ex*-best friend.**
26   **NED: C'mon, Raff, what are you talkin' about?**
27   **RAFF: You know what I'm talkin' about. Tonight at the lodge**
28   **meetin' when they took the vote to see who should take the**
29   **money home to buy refreshments, *you* stood up and said I**
30   **shouldn't get it.**
31   **NED: Well, that's right, Raff, 'cause whenever you take the**
32   **refreshment money home wit' you, you always spend it on**
33   **something else, and then we don't got no refreshments.**
34   **RAFF: I wasn't gonna take the money and spend it.**
35   **NED: Sure you was. You do it all the time.**

1   RAFF: No I don't.
2   NED: That's what you said last time.
3   RAFF: But that was an emergency.
4   NED: Yeah, that's what you always say.
5   RAFF: But this time I really will pay it back.
6   NED: There, you see?
7   RAFF: But this time really is an emergency. You know who's
8   waitin' for me downstairs with Allie?
9   NED: Tricky?
10   RAFF: No, not Tricky. My mother-in-law!
11   NED: You mean the female Godzilla?
12   RAFF: That's right. Today's her birthday, and we're supposed to
13   take her out for dinner.
14   NED: But Raff, I thought you hated your mother-in-law.
15   RAFF: I do, Morton, more than anything else in the world. That's
16   why I gotta take her out.
17   NED: So why don't Allie just get her somethin'? It's her mother!
18   RAFF: Because she called Allie last week and told her she wanted
19   to go to some fancy restaurant downtown.
20   NED: So why don'tcha just go and get it over with?
21   RAFF: 'Cause I used up all my money buyin' a new bowlin' ball
22   yesterday to replace the one you dropped out the window.
23   NED: Don't blame me, the ball just slipped off my hand. I can't
24   help it you got fat fingers. Hee, hee. You gotta admit that ball
25   bounced pretty good, huh?
26   RAFF: Almost hit that policeman on the head.
27   NED: Yeah. Boy, was he mad! Hey, too bad *he* wasn't your mother-
28   in-law. Then you wouldn't have no problem!
29   RAFF: Yeah? Well, I do. *(RAFF begins to pace.)* I gotta figure out a
30   way to get my hands on some quick dough.
31   NED: You know, Raff, what you need is a miracle.
32   RAFF: A what?
33   NED: A miracle. You know, like when Jesus fed the five thousand
34   with a couple of fish.
35   RAFF: It'll never work, Morton. I ain't even got enough cash for a

1   couple of fish sticks. Besides, that stuff don't really happen
2   anyway.
3   NED: C'mon, Raff, what about _____ *(Insert an*
4   *unbelievable current event)* **or the '69 Mets, or ...** *(NED takes a*
5   *small card out of his pocket.)* **Or one of these.**
6   RAFF: What's that?
7   NED: It's a lottery ticket, Raff. I bought it last week. All's we got to
8   do is rub off the numbers and cash it in.
9   RAFF: What are you, nuts? No one ever wins those things.
10   NED: That's the problem, Raff — you gotta believe in these things.
11   You never win 'cause you got no faith. But I'm tellin' ya, this
12   baby's a winner. *(NED scratches the card.)* What'd I tell ya?
13   We got ourselves a winner!
14   RAFF: Lemme see that thing. *(RAFF grabs the card.)*
15   NED: Park Avenue, here we come!
16   RAFF: *Ahhh, ahhhh, AHHHH! Two dollars?!*
17   NED: That's right. It's an instant winner.
18   RAFF: Two dollars? How's that gonna help?
19   NED: Well, we could use it to go down and buy two more tickets, so
20   we can ...
21   RAFF: Would you cut that out? This has gone far enough. There's
22   only one thing to do.
23   NED: Yeah, well, maybe you're right.
24   RAFF: You know it. I'll just have to stay here at your place until
25   my mother-in-law leaves.
26   NED: But Raff, I ain't got enough food for you to stay here.
27   Besides, what do I tell Allie?
28   RAFF: Oh yeah, Allie. Hey! I got it. *(RAFF grabs the phone and*
29   *dials.)*
30   NED: Whatcha doin'?
31   RAFF: You're gonna tell her I been kidnapped. *(RAFF gives NED*
32   *the phone.)*
33   NED: But Raff, I can't ... Oh, hello, Allie. This is Ned Morton from
34   upstairs. Oh, you do? *(He covers the phone.)* **She recognized**
35   **my voice.**

1   **RAFF: Would you get on with it?**
2   **NED: Hey, Allie, I'm callin' you on account of Raff got kidnapped**
3   **after the lodge meetin' tonight.** *(Pause)* **Who done it? Where is**
4   **he? How much do they want? I dunno, ah, I'll have to ask**
5   **him. Hey, Raff ...** *(RAFF grabs the phone and does a slow*
6   *burn.)*
7   **RAFF:** *(Mimicking NED)* **I'll ask him! Humph!** *(Into the phone)* **Hi,**
8   **honey. Boy, the Morton's some kidder, huh? Me? I'm fine.**
9   **How's your mother? She is? She did? That's great!**
10   **NED: What — she in the hospital? Hee hee.**
11   **RAFF:** *(Still into the phone)* **OK, I'll be right down.** *(He hangs up.)*
12   **Hey Morton, guess what? Allie's mother won a hundred**
13   **dollars in the lottery, and she wants to take us out to dinner**
14   **tonight.**
15   **NED: That's great, Raff, but you're still gonna need a miracle.**
16   **There's no way she could feed you for less than a hundred**
17   **dollars!** *(NED "hee-hees," then he and RAFF head for the door.*
18   *NED exits, but RAFF pauses and thoughtfully looks toward*
19   *heaven.)*
20   **RAFF: You know, maybe I do got someone up there watchin' out**
21   **for me. Maybe Morton's right — maybe I should be more**
22   **thankful. God, you're the greatest!** *(RAFF exits.)*
23
24
25
26
27
28
29
30
31
32
33
34
35

Hairaldo — Putting the Psych Back in Psychic

By Dan Rupple

Cast: Hairaldo; Panel — Student (college-aged), Mystic (middle-aged woman), Angry Man (thirtyish), Psychic, extras for the studio audience.

Setting: The set of the television show *Hairaldo*. There should be four chairs set up in a row at Stage Left. At Stage Right should be chairs for the studio audience.

Props: None.

Costumes: A suit with a tie and a black "big hair" wig for Hairaldo. Everyone else may be dressed casually.

1　*(HAIRALDO stands in the middle of his studio audience. The*
2　*panel — STUDENT, MYSTIC, ANGRY MAN and PSYCHIC — is*
3　*seated off to the side.)*
4　**HAIRALDO:** **Hi, I'm Hairaldo Rivera. How would you like a**
5　**religion where good and evil disappears? A religion that helps**
6　**you realize that you are the center of the universe? That you**
7　**are God? Welcome to the New Age. It's everywhere —**
8　**psychics, reincarnation, crystals. But is it new? Or is it ancient**
9　**Eastern mysticism, westernized by Hollywood machinery?**
10　**New Age putting the *psych* back in psychic, on this edition of**
11　***Hairaldo.***
12　**STUDENT:** *(Disgruntled)* **This New Age teacher tells me that**
13　**meditation and trances and biofeedback are the doors of**
14　**perception. That he is the prime reality, the center of the**
15　**universe, that he is God! Then we take a break, and he never**
16　**comes back. This Center of the Universe can't even find his**
17　**way out of the men's room!** *(HAIRALDO poses a question to the*
18　*MYSTIC on the panel.)*
19　**HAIRALDO: Now, Christianity relies on the proven truth of the**
20　**holy Scriptures. What do you base your beliefs on?**
21　**MYSTIC: Oh, well, we have our sacred writings.**
22　**HAIRALDO: For instance?**
23　**MYSTIC: Well, … we have the Shirley MacLaine books … and**
24　**some novels … and someone told me if you interpret them just**
25　**right, the early works of The Three Stooges.**
26　**ANGRY MAN: I hear of people being kings in past lives, being**
27　**famous explorers, having past exciting, romantic adventures.**
28　**Well, I go to crystal ball brain here** *(Points to PSYCHIC next to*
29　*him),* **and you know what he says? He tells me I shoveled hay**
30　**for the pony express, I cleaned Cleopatra's swimming pool**
31　**and I was Benedict Arnold's barber.**
32　**PSYCHIC: You paid for the special. What do you expect for**
33　**$18.95?**
34　**ANGRY MAN:** *(Starts to physically attack PSYCHIC.)* **You better**
35　**start expecting my fist through your nose!**

1	HAIRALDO: Hey, settle down. I don't need any more broken
2	noses.
3	ANGRY MAN: Who cares? There's no right or wrong. *(Pointing to*
4	*PSYCHIC)* He taught me that. *(To PSYCHIC)* You're the center
5	of the universe. Where's your new reality now?
6	HAIRALDO: The New Age — a deceptive philosophy, as slippery
7	as a wet pig. The New Age — putting the *psych* back in
8	psychic ... right here on *Hairaldo.*
9	
10	
11	
12	
13	
14	
15	
16	
17	
18	
19	
20	
21	
22	
23	
24	
25	
26	
27	
28	
29	
30	
31	
32	
33	
34	
35	

Hammer

By Dan Rupple, Dave Toole and Larry Watt

Cast: Thompson, Watt, Smith.

Setting: A home improvement store. Place a table at Center Stage to hold all the props except the hammer.

Props: A board, nails, newspaper, hammer, rubber band, cup, sandwich.

Costumes: Jeans and T-shirts, perhaps with look-alike caps from a home improvement store. Thompson has a bandage on his hand.

1   *(THOMPSON and WATT stand at the table. THOMPSON holds a*
2   *board.)*
3   THOMPSON: OK, Watt, this is your area. Now all you have to do
4   is put these nails *(Picks up nails)* in the board.
5   WATT: In the board?
6   THOMPSON: That's right, just drive them in the board. *(Sets*
7   *board and nails on the table.)* If you have any questions, just ask
8   Smith over there — *(Points)* he used to be in nails. I'm going
9   to lunch. I'll be back in about an hour to see how you're doing.
10   *(Leaves.)*
11   WATT: In the board, huh? *(Tries all kinds of ways to drive in the*
12   *nails. Uses his fist, head and a newspaper.)*
13   SMITH: Hi.
14   WATT: Hi.
15   SMITH: Whatcha doing?
16   WATT: I'm driving these nails into the board.
17   SMITH: Well, I've got this hammer here. You're welcome to it.
18   WATT: No, that's OK; I'm doing fine. *(Tries newspaper again, then*
19   *rubber band.)*
20   SMITH: Well, it works great. I've got it right here.
21   WATT: No thanks, I don't need it.
22   SMITH: Well, I'll tell you what — I'll just leave it here in case you
23   change your mind. *(Leaves hammer on table, then exits. WATT*
24   *tries a cup and a sandwich, then finally tries the hammer. It*
25   *works! He pounds in three nails. THOMPSON enters.)*
26   THOMPSON: *(Picks up board.)* Wow, all three of them! That's
27   great! How'd you do it?
28   WATT: With a hammer!
29   THOMPSON: Oh yeah, Smith give you that? Yeah, he uses one,
30   but none of us use them. *(Shows bandaged hand.)* They're just
31   a crutch. You don't need them.
32
33
34
35

134

Hardness of Heart Foundation

By Dan Rupple

Cast: Doctor, Lester Boggs.

Setting: A television studio. Place a podium at Center Stage.

Props: None.

Costumes: A lab coat for the Doctor and a suit and tie for Lester.

1   *(DOCTOR and LESTER stand at a podium Center Stage.)*
2   DOCTOR: And now Lester Boggs, on behalf of the Hardness of
3   Heart Foundation.
4   LESTER: Hi, I'm Lester Boggs. You probably remember me best
5   from those frolicking scenes on *Hugo's Hangout*. Lots of
6   chuckles in those old shows. But today I'd like to speak to you
7   about something much more serious.
8   Did you know that in our country today one of the major
9   causes of eternal death is hardness of heart? Right now, as you
10   sit there listening to my voice, you could be in more danger
11   than you realize. Now I know many of you are saying, Lester
12   buddy, what are you talking about? You're thinking, I don't
13   even know what hardness of heart is, let alone if I have it or
14   not.
15   Well, let me give you an example. Quite a few years ago I
16   was out on the farm, walking in the field with one of the mules.
17   Well, it came time to turn around and head back to the barn.
18   So I started pulling on this old mule, trying to start her home,
19   but she wanted to go on. Now I knew a little further in the
20   direction that mule wanted to go was a huge open pit and at
21   the bottom ... oooo-eeee! Snakes, black widows, insurance
22   salesmen and countless other critters that I sure wouldn't call
23   neighbor. But that old mule was determined to head that way
24   and resisted me pulling her back home. No matter what I said
25   to her, she just ignored my voice. I think after a while she
26   didn't even hear me. Well, I kept pulling, and then suddenly
27   the rope broke and off ran that old mule, heading toward the
28   hole, then *whammo* — she gets hit by a two-ton semi truck.
29   Oh, I didn't tell you, the hole was on the other side of a
30   freeway, which only goes to show ya — you never know about
31   tomorrow. If only she hadn't been so stubborn.
32   And you know, each day millions of people enter into
33   eternal death that could have been avoided if only they had
34   heeded the pull of the Spirit.
35   DOCTOR: Thank you, Lester. Yes, it's so simple. No rigid

1   exercises. God himself will take that heart of stone and
2   replace it with a heart of flesh. Just one easy step, and you are
3   immediately transformed from an eternal bout with death to
4   everlasting life with Jesus Christ. And upkeep? Just a steady
5   diet of God's Word — a virtual feast, and not an ounce of fat.
6   Friend, I urge you: put away those things that make your
7   heart a walking time bomb. They're not worth it. Let the joy
8   of the Lord rule in your heart. Remember, a merry heart is
9   like good medicine, but hardness of heart is no laughing
10   matter. So if you're suffering from hardness of heart, be sure
11   to make an immediate appointment with the Great Physician.
12   Like Lester Boggs says …
13 **LESTER:** *Whammo!*
14 **DOCTOR:** It's later than you think.
15
16
17
18
19
20
21
22
23
24
25
26
27
28
29
30
31
32
33
34
35

Heavenly Home Travel Bureau

By Dan Rupple

Cast: Announcer, Travel Agent, Man, Young Lady, Heaven's Agent, Lady, Yuppie (male).

Setting: A travel agency at Stage Right and Heaven's gate at Stage Left.

Props: Magazine for Man, photos for Young Lady, card saying "Jesus" for Lady.

Costumes: The only special costume needed is an angel costume for Heaven's Agent.

1   *(TRAVEL AGENT sits at desk. MAN paging through magazine*
2   *and YOUNG LADY looking at photos sit on chairs at either side.)*
3   **ANNOUNCER:** *(From Off-stage)* **If the cares of this world are**
4   **taking away your joy, look up — start planning now for your**
5   **eternal vacation.**
6   **TRAVEL AGENT: Welcome to the Heavenly Home Travel Bureau.**
7   **We're here to help you get started now in preparing for that**
8   **great day.**
9   **MAN:** *(Looking at his magazine)* **Wow, these mansions are**
10   **incredible, but I could never afford it.**
11   **TRAVEL AGENT: Sure you can … on the layaway plan. Start**
12   **doing everything you can for the kingdom now!**
13   **YOUNG LADY:** *(Showing photo to MAN)* **See this chandelier? I got**
14   **that from volunteering at the rescue mission.**
15   **MAN: Wow, that's incredible! These places look like someone's**
16   **been working on them for over two thousand years!** *(All*
17   *laugh.)*
18   **TRAVEL AGENT: That's right, while Jesus is preparing Heaven**
19   **for you, prepare yourself for Heaven. We'll teach you the local**
20   **language, otherwise known as prayer, and you'll learn the**
21   **local customs, like singing hymns and praise songs. And the**
22   **most important point of all, we'll help you make sure that**
23   **your credentials are in perfect order.** *(HEAVEN'S AGENT*
24   *enters Stage Left. LADY and YUPPIE enter and stand to the side*
25   *of HEAVEN'S AGENT, with LADY being first in line.)*
26   **HEAVEN'S AGENT: May I see your passport, please?**
27   **LADY: No problem. Here it is.** *(She shows a card that simply says*
28   *"Jesus.")*
29   **HEAVEN'S AGENT: Welcome.**
30   **YUPPIE: What? I don't have one of those. Don't you take**
31   **American Express? How about Diner's Club?**
32   **HEAVEN'S AGENT: I'm sorry.** *(LADY and HEAVEN'S AGENT exit*
33   *Stage Left. YUPPIE exits in a different direction.)*
34   **TRAVEL AGENT: Be prepared for that glorious day. Your**
35   **heavenly home: No more sorrow, no more sin, just joyous**

1 peace and continual fellowship. Make your reservations now.
2 It may be later than you think.
3 ANNOUNCER: *(From Off-stage)* Call now for your free gift of
4 grace. Offer void where prohibited by the law.
5
6
7
8
9
10
11
12
13
14
15
16
17
18
19
20
21
22
23
24
25
26
27
28
29
30
31
32
33
34
35

Hogwash Jeopardy

By Dan Rupple

Cast: Phil Newberry, Ed Lardo, Joe Parker, Hooto Crunk.

Setting: A television game show set. Place two podiums at Center Stage.

Props: Hogwash Jeopardy board (optional — may be mimed), two cards, two markers. The Hogwash Jeopardy board may be a piece of posterboard with a grid drawn on it of four squares across and four squares down (sixteen total squares). Across the top row should be the four categories: Geology on Other Planets, As Rumor Has It, Celebrity Wisdom, and Foods Beginning with the Letter C. The second Row should have a 10 in each box; the third row a 20 in each box; and the fourth row, a 30 in each box. (See example.)

Geology on Other Planets	As Rumor Has It	Celebrity Wisdom	Foods Beginning with the Letter C
10	10	10	10
20	20	20	20
30	30	30	30

Costumes: Suit and tie for Phil. Casual clothes for Joe and Hooto. Hooto may also wear goofy glasses.

Sound Effects: Buzzer, ring, music.

Notes: Crowd noise may be taped.

1   ED: *(From Off-stage)* **It's time for** *Hogwash Jeopardy,* **the game**
2   **where you decide: Is it truth or is it hogwash? And here's the**
3   **host of** *Hogwash Jeopardy,* **Phil Newberry.** *(Applause as PHIL*
4   *enters and stands at Center Stage.)*
5   PHIL: **Thank you, Ed Lardo, and hello to you out there. Welcome**
6   **to another thrilling game of** *Hogwash Jeopardy.* **Before we go**
7   **any further, let's meet this week's contestants. Ed?**
8   ED: **Phil, our first contestant is the father of two small children, as**
9   **well as the manager of a shoe store in Seattle, Washington. He**
10   **likes to spend his spare time at sporting events and at church**
11   **activities. Phil, meet Joe Parker.** *(Applause as JOE enters and*
12   *stands at his podium.)*
13 PHIL: **So, Joe, two children. What are their ages?**
14 JOE: **Well, my boy is five and our girl is two.**
15 PHIL: **Great, and which one is the oldest?**
16 JOE: **The boy, Phil.**
17 PHIL: **The boy, the boy indeed. Well, good to have you here, and**
18   **good luck to you.**
19 JOE: **Thank you, Phil.**
20 ED: **And luck he'll need, Phil, as we meet our six-time champion,**
21   **playing in his fourteenth straight** *Hogwash Jeopardy.* **Phil, you**
22   **know him by now. From Woonsocket, Rhode Island, audience,**
23   **please welcome Hooto Crunk.** *(Applause as HOOTO enters and*
24   *stands at his podium.)*
25 PHIL: **Well, back once again. Gonna give it another try?**
26 HOOTO: **That's right, Phil. I'm rarin' to go.**
27 PHIL: **Well then, let's get started. As you know, contestants, our**
28   *Hogwash Jeopardy* **board is divided into four categories, and**
29   **each category is divided into three more sections for ten,**
30   **twenty and thirty points. When you pick your category, a**
31   **statement will appear. You will either complete the statement**
32   **or state if it is true or if it is hogwash.**
33 HOOTO: **Those are the fun ones.**
34 PHIL: **Should you answer the question wrong, your opponent may**
35   **hit his buzzer and answer correctly. The contestant scoring**

142

1   the most points at the end of the game is the winner. Any
2   questions?
3 JOE: No, I think I got it.
4 HOOTO: Piece of cake.
5 PHIL: OK, let's flip our *Hogwash Jeopardy* board and reveal
6   today's categories. *(Turns board around.)* They are: Geology on
7   Other Planets, As Rumor Has It, Celebrity Wisdom, and
8   Foods Beginning with the Letter C. Hooto, you won the toss
9   backstage, so you begin.
10 HOOTO: Thank you, Phil. I'll take Celebrity Wisdom for twenty.
11 PHIL: Don't you mean for ten?
12 HOOTO: No, twenty. It's a Crunk tradition — you know, like
13   changing the air in your tires on Christmas Eve.
14 PHIL: OK, that sounds good enough to me. In a recent letter to
15   President Reagan, this television star advised the president of
16   a fail-proof six-point plan to world peace.
17 HOOTO: Who is LaVerne DeFazio?
18 PHIL: LaVerne DeFazio it is. Please continue, Hooto.
19 HOOTO: I'll go for Celebrity Wisdom for thirty.
20 PHIL: Because of his fascinating topics and intelligent discussions,
21   Phil Donahue is the most respected man on daytime television.
22 HOOTO: Hogwash! Who is Richard Simmons?
23 PHIL: Yes.
24 HOOTO: I'm gonna go for As Rumor Has It for ten.
25 PHIL: As rumor has it, when billionaire Howard Hughes died,
26   approximately how much money did he leave behind?
27 HOOTO: Uh, uh-oh, uh, what is four-and-a-half billion dollars?
28 PHIL: No, I'm sorry. *(JOE hits his buzzer.)* Joe?
29 JOE: What is all of it? Just like everyone else, Phil.
30 PHIL: All of it, yes indeed. A correct answer. You now control the
31   board, Joe. Go ahead.
32 JOE: I'll take As Rumor Has It for twenty.
33 PHIL: The role of James Bond was made famous on screen by Sean
34   Connery. As rumor has it, who was originally offered this
35   role?

143

1   JOE: Who was Dom DeLuise?

2   PHIL: Dom DeLuise it is.

3   HOOTO: Come on — that's an easy one.

4   PHIL: Go ahead, Joe.

5   JOE: OK, I'll take Foods Beginning With the Letter C for ten.

6   PHIL: This food means cold, reminds you of hot, and is found in

7   South America.

8   JOE: Uh, what is coffee?

9   PHIL: No, I'm sorry. *(HOOTO hits his buzzer.)* Hooto?

10 HOOTO: What is chili?

11 PHIL: Chili. Yes, indeed.

12 HOOTO: I'm gonna go for Geology on Other Planets for ten.

13 PHIL: Top of the board ...

14 HOOTO: See, chili is hot, but ...

15 PHIL: Which planet is closest to Pluto?

16 HOOTO: Uh, what?

17 PHIL: Closest to Pluto?

18 HOOTO: Who is Donald Duck?

19 PHIL: No.

20 HOOTO: Daffy Duck!

21 PHIL: No, we're looking for a planet. *(JOE presses buzzer.)* Joe?

22 JOE: What is Neptune?

23 PHIL: That's right. Please continue, Joe.

24 JOE: OK, same category for twenty.

25 PHIL: Dookie originated on ... *(Ring)* Oh, time's up. We go into our

26   Final Hogwash Jeopardy with the score of Joe Parker, forty

27   points, and Hooto Crunk again in the lead with sixty points.

28   This question is worth fifty points. A correct answer, and Joe,

29   you could go into first place, and Hooto, you could win your

30   seventh championship.

31 HOOTO: In the bag.

32 PHIL: Our category is Eternal Truths. Our question is from the

33   Bible. In the New Testament a rich young ruler approaches

34   Jesus and asks, "Good Master, what must I do to inherit

35   eternal life" (Mark 10:17, author's paraphrase)? Writing on the

1   cards in front of you, what was Jesus' reply? *(Music plays as*
2   *HOOTO and JOE write their answers on their cards.)* **OK, time's**
3   **up. Hooto, to clinch first place.**
4 **HOOTO:** *(Displaying his card)* **He said, "No problemo! With a suit**
5   **like that, there's no way God's gonna keep you out."**
6 **PHIL: Oh, I'm sorry, that's not right. Joe Parker, we go to you!**
7 **JOE:** *(Displaying his card)* **He said, "You lack one thing. Sell all that**
8   **you have, give to the poor and come, follow me"** (Mark 10:21,
9   author's paraphrase).
10 **PHIL: Yes, that's right. Joe you're our new champion, defeating**
11   **Hooto Crunk ninety points to sixty. Joe, any comment?**
12 **JOE: Well, I guess when it finally comes down to it, it's not just**
13   *what* **you know, but** *who* **you know.**
14 **PHIL: Good point, and that's about all the time we have for now.**
15   **See ya next time on *Hogwash Jeopardy.*** *(Optional theme music)*
16 **HOOTO: Who do you know? The producer?**
17
18
19
20
21
22
23
24
25
26
27
28
29
30
31
32
33
34
35

Is It Worth the Price?

By Dan Rupple

Cast: Announcer, Jim Kennedy, Ken Lankey, Gilbert Duckland, Volunteer.

Setting: The television set of a game show. Place a podium at Center Stage and hang up the three boards (described below).

Props: A snapshot, the board (which in its simplest form may be a large pad of paper or dry erase board on which are written "Shut the Door" and later "Save Her"), the Prize Board (may be made of cardboard, possibly decorated with glitter, with "Prize Board" lettered on top and an envelope with a slip of paper inside attached), the Grim Reaper Board (made of cardboard that is painted black, with "Grim Reaper Board" lettered on top and an envelope with a slip of paper inside attached), three water balloons.

Costumes: Suit and tie for Jim. Casual clothing for the others.

Sound Effects: Clock ticking and buzz.

Notes: Crowd noise may be taped.

1   *(Optional theme music plays.)*
2 ANNOUNCER: *(From Off-stage)* **Welcome to *Is It Worth the Price?* —**
3   **the game where there's a price to be paid for every choice, and**
4   **we're here to see if it's worth that price.** And now, here's your
5   **host, Jim Kennedy.** *(JIM enters to applause.)*
6 JIM: **Thank you, studio audience, and welcome to all of you**
7   **viewing at home. Once again we have two contestants willing**
8   **to put it all on the line to see if their choices are worth the**
9   **price. Let's meet our first contestant.**
10 ANNOUNCER: **Jim, our first contestant is Ken Lankey. Ken, come**
11   **on down!** *(KEN enters and stands at a podium.)*
12 JIM: **Welcome to the show, Ken. Where are you from?**
13 KEN: **I'm from Chicago, Illinois.**
14 JIM: **Oh, the Windy City. What do you do there?**
15 KEN: **I'm a drill press salesman.**
16 JIM: **Are you married, Ken?**
17 KEN: **Yes, I've been married for eight years, and we have seven**
18   **children.**
19 JIM: **OK, Ken, do you know how to play *Is It Worth The Price?***
20 KEN: **Sure do. You give me a situation, and if my choice is worth**
21   **the price, I go to the Prize Board; and if my choice isn't, I go**
22   **to the Grim Reaper Board.**
23 JIM: **That's right, Ken, so let's play *Is It Worth the Price?* Your**
24   **category is "faithfulness."**
25 KEN: **Oh, my gosh. I hope the kids aren't watching.**
26 JIM: **Do you travel much on business?**
27 KEN: **As a matter of fact, I have out-of-town meetings every month.**
28 JIM: **OK, here is your situation: You're on a long business trip. It's**
29   **late at night, and you're sitting in your lonely hotel room when**
30   **an attractive young lady knocks on the door. Here's a**
31   **snapshot, Ken.**
32 KEN: *(Looks.)* **Oh, baby!**
33 JIM: **Wishing to come in, she offers you quite a proposition, and**
34   **I'm not talking about Parcheesi. What do you do, Ken? Is**
35   **asking her in worth the price?**

1   KEN: Can I see the picture again?

2   JIM: Sure. *(Shows snapshot to KEN.)*

3   KEN: Oh, my gosh!

4   JIM: It's up to you, Ken. Audience? *(There is the sound of a clock*

5   *ticking, then a buzz.)* All right, Ken, what will it be?

6   KEN: You sure it'll be that girl?

7   JIM: Yes siree, Ken.

8   KEN: I'd say no and shut the door.

9   JIM: You'd shut the door, so you say it wasn't worth the price.

10   Let's look at the board. It says "Shut the Door."

11   KEN: All right, not that I'm interested, but if I had opened the

12   door, what would've happened?

13   JIM: Well, three months later, the young lady sues you and wins a

14   lucrative paternity suit.

15   KEN: Is that anything like a three-piece suit?

16   JIM: In the divorce settlement, you lose the house and all visitation

17   rights. Soon you are known to your children simply as

18   "Slimehead." Brokenhearted and filled with guilt, you turn to

19   alcohol, and soon your home address is the riverbed.

20   KEN: What a bummer!

21   JIM: But you chose to shut the door, and your decision earns you,

22   Ken Lankey, a trip to our Prize Board.

23   KEN: OK. *(KEN gets envelope from Prize Board and removes slip of*

24   *paper.)*

25   JIM: Ken, you have just won a trip for two to Puerto Vallarta!

26   KEN: Oh boy, and I don't even speak French.

27   JIM: OK, yes, Ken, you made the right choice, because it wasn't

28   worth the price.

29   KEN: Thank you, Jim. It was tough, but it seemed like the right

30   thing to do. I mean, I made a commitment to the little woman.

31   JIM: Indeed you did — seven kids' worth. Thanks for being with

32   us.

33   KEN: Jim, I'll be thinking of you when we're snow skiing in Puerto

34   Vallarta. Thanks so much.

35   JIM: Not at all. *(KEN exits.)* Now let's meet our second contestant.

1   ANNOUNCER: Jim, our next contestant is Gilbert Duckland.
2   **Gilbert, come on down!** *(GILBERT enters and stands at the*
3   *podium.)*
4   JIM: Hello, Gilbert, and welcome to *Is It Worth the Price?*
5   GILBERT: Thank you, Mr. Kennedy.
6   JIM: Where are you from, Gilbert?
7   GILBERT: Oh, I was just sitting out there in the audience.
8   JIM: No, I mean where do you live?
9   GILBERT: Oh! Like on a regular basis. Um, Del Rio, Nevada. That
10   means "from the river." Although I'm not from the river, I'm
11   just from Del Rio.
12   JIM: OK, Gilbert, let's begin. Your category is "revenge."
13   GILBERT: Sounds like fun.
14   JIM: Well, we'll see. I understand that you have a certain sister-in-
15   law that you don't get along with too well.
16   GILBERT: That'd be Norma.
17   JIM: When did this hostility begin?
18   GILBERT: Jim, it all goes back to when she didn't want me to
19   marry her sister. And after I asked her to be my best man.
20   JIM: Have you had any recent problems with Norma?
21   GILBERT: Sure. Just last Saturday I was working in my driveway,
22   and that old witch parks her broom right on my tool box.
23   JIM: She drives a broom?
24   GILBERT: Well, she says it's a Buick, but a broom's more her
25   speed.
26   JIM: I think we get the picture.
27   GILBERT: Now my tool box is as flat as her head. It was a
28   Craftsman, too.
29   JIM: OK, here's your situation. You are hiking with Norma.
30   Suddenly she slips over the edge of a huge cliff.
31   GILBERT: I like it.
32   JIM: She grabs for a small branch and clutches it. Then she calls
33   you to pull her back to safety. Precious seconds pass as the
34   branch begins to break. Gilbert, here is your decision: You are
35   the only one who can save her, but you remember how much

1   you dislike her.

2   GILBERT: That's not hard.

3   JIM: Gilbert, is letting her drop worth the price? Audience? *(There*

4   *is a sound of a clock ticking and then a buzz.)* OK, what do you

5   say?

6   GILBERT: I'd drop her like a hot potato.

7   JIM: You'd let her go?

8   GILBERT: Maybe then she'll know how my tool box feels — all

9   squashed.

10   JIM: Let's look at the board. Oh, Gilbert, it says "Save Her." It

11   wasn't worth the price.

12   GILBERT: Big deal. Who wants to save Moby Dick?

13   JIM: Well, you go to the Grim Reaper Board. *(GILBERT removes*

14   *the envelope from the Grim Reaper Board and removes the slip of*

15   *paper.)* I'm going to need a volunteer from the audience.

16   *(VOLUNTEER comes forward as JIM explains.)* If you let her

17   drop at the end of the fall, she smashes the windshield of your

18   car parked below. That earns you a remorse balloon. Let her

19   fly. *(VOLUNTEER throws water balloon at GILBERT.)* The good

20   news is, you're insured. The bad news is, Norma lives. That

21   earns another balloon. *(VOLUNTEER throws second water*

22   *balloon.)* Norma presses charges and wins, and you spend

23   fifteen years in prison.

24   GILBERT: You got a rain coat?

25   JIM: That earns you another balloon. *(VOLUNTEER throws third*

26   *water balloon.)*

27   GILBERT: Boy, of all the luck.

28   JIM: No, Gilbert, it wasn't worth the price. Looks like you lost.

29   GILBERT: I've been losing all my life. I think that Norma cursed

30   me or something. *(As he exits)* I knew she was a witch.

31   JIM: Well, Gilbert Duckland took matters into his own hands, and

32   I guess revenge isn't worth the price. We're about out of time.

33   This is Jim Kennedy, reminding you that before you make a

34   decision, ask yourself: Is it worth the price? Good day!

35   *(Optional theme music)*

Montague — Call of the Wild

By Dan Rupple

Cast: Announcer, Phil Montague, Gus Hunt, Audience Member (female), Caller.

Setting: A TV talk show. Two chairs are at Center Stage, angling in toward each other.

Props: None.

Costumes: Phil Montague wears big glasses, a white or gray hairpiece and a suit and tie. Gus wears camping clothing.

Sound Effects: Optional theme music.

1   ANNOUNCER: *(From Off-stage)* And now, live, America's foremost
2   audience participation talk show, *Montague*. And here's your
3   host, Phil Montague. *(PHIL enters.)*
4   PHIL: Before we get started today, I'd like to see by your applause
5   how many would agree that man has a role and lifestyle that
6   he was created for? *(Pause.)* OK, how about the concept that
7   like any other species of animal, humankind can live by any
8   code that we decide to adopt? *(Pause.)* Well, if you're like me,
9   from the first time you saw Tarzan, you were fascinated by the
10   possibility of a human being raised from infancy by wild
11   animals. Well, as far as today's guest is concerned, this is not
12   a possibility but a reality. My guest is Gus Hunt, a man like
13   you or me, except for the slight misfortune that he was raised
14   by wild ducks. Mr. Hunt, welcome to the show. *(GUS enters.)*
15   GUS: Thank you, Phil. I really appreciate you having me on. *(PHIL*
16   *and GUS sit.)*
17   PHIL: Now Gus, you claim to have been raised by wild ducks.
18   GUS: That is correct. From the time I was a year old, the only
19   parents I knew had webbed feet and honkers that'd put Jamie
20   Farr to shame.
21   PHIL: How did your incredible circumstance come about?
22   GUS: I was riding in the back of my daddy's pickup a few miles
23   from our farm when my dad hit a bump, and darned if I
24   didn't just bounce right on out of the truck.
25   PHIL: Didn't your parents come back for you?! I mean, come on —
26   as a society, where is our sense of responsibility?
27   GUS: Well, they were pretty busy with the farm and all, but sure,
28   they searched a couple of months later. 'Course by that time,
29   I was more duck than human.
30   PHIL: How did you first enter the duck lifestyle?
31   GUS: As I lay there by the side of the road, fearing that at any
32   moment I could become a hood ornament, a rather large
33   female duck waddled up and rolled me with her beak to her
34   nest. There she literally took me under her wing as her very
35   own.

1   PHIL: Were there times that you felt different, alienated from the
2   other ducks?
3   GUS: Oh, sure.
4   PHIL: So they treated you like an outcast?
5   GUS: No, they flew south for the winter. I never made it beyond
6   Cleveland. *(Phil points mic at female audience member.)*
7   AUDIENCE MEMBER: Did all of this, I mean, being an ugly
8   duckling, so to speak, damage your self-esteem?
9   GUS: No, it didn't really ruffle my feathers. 'Course I come from
10   a very prestigious duck background. My uncle on my
11   mother's side was Daffy.
12   PHIL: Now that's fascinating. Daffy duck from cartoon fame?!
13   GUS: No, just Daffy. He was as crazy as they come. This duck
14   would play chicken with a 747. Then there was my great-
15   grandfather, the famous Native American, Sitting Duck. My
16   brother, the doctor, we're ashamed of …
17   PHIL: Oh?
18   GUS: Yeah, a real quack. And my grandfather tried his wing at
19   politics.
20   PHIL: Not much success?
21   GUS: No, he hurt his foot and, as you know, no one ever elects a
22   lame duck.
23   PHIL: Now how did your return to manhood come about?
24   GUS: Well, one day when I was about twenty-one years old, I was
25   discovered by a group of missionaries.
26   PHIL: Missionaries! OK, so now you're gonna tell us that they
27   made you repent from this evil lifestyle and converted you to
28   God's high and mighty plan for your life?
29   GUS: Not at all, Phil. They just said, "You ain't no duck."
30   PHIL: OK, let me get this straight. You feel that it is wrong and
31   abnormal for a person to have a different lifestyle, but tell the
32   truth — after all those years, good years, as a duck, wouldn't
33   you even consider going back?
34   GUS: No way! The truth is, to make sense of this world and to
35   ultimately survive it, a person has to live the life that was

1   created for him. You can't buck God's design and not crack
2   up. Or in my case … quack up!
3   PHIL: Now come on. Isn't that an extremely limited view of what
4   mankind is really all about? I mean, to say that it is unnatural
5   for a man to be a duck if he so desires is the same kind of
6   prejudice that says a woman can't be a father, that two men
7   can't share the same toothbrush, or even that my daughter
8   can't grow a mustache!
9   GUS: Your daughter has a mustache?
10   PHIL: No, of course not; that's just an example. Although Marlo
11   has a little … oh, never mind! Is the caller there?
12   CALLER: I just wanted to say, I agree with your guest. I think that
13   it's enough of a challenge trying to become who you're
14   supposed to be, let alone someone you're not. Which makes
15   me wonder, what kinds of problems does Gus have adjusting
16   to his life as a human?
17   GUS: You're right, it's always a struggle. The other day I saw a row
18   of down jackets at K-Mart, and I went crazy. I must have
19   known seventy percent of them. I don't even want to mention
20   feather dusters. Ewww — I get the chills just thinking about it.
21   PHIL: OK, well, we're about out of time. Gus, where do you go
22   from here? Are you going to become some crusader?
23   GUS: No, Phil, starting tomorrow, I'll be barricading myself in my
24   bathtub for about a month.
25   PHIL: Why's that?
26   GUS: It's hunting season.
27   PHIL: I see. Well, good luck to you, and thanks for being here. And
28   thank you, ladies and gentlemen, for your questions and
29   opinions.
30   ANNOUNCER: *(From Off-stage)* You've been watching *The Phil*
31   *Montague Show*, brought to you by Miss Clearhold hair
32   spray — hair spray of the stars. Marlo uses it, and so does
33   Phil. *(Optional theme music plays.)*
34
35

Montague — Presenting Noah

By Dan Rupple

Cast: Announcer, Phil Montague, Noah, Caller.

Setting: A TV talk show. Two chairs are at Center Stage, angling in toward each other.

Props: An umbrella.

Costumes: Phil Montague wears big glasses, a white or gray hairpiece and a suit and tie. Noah wears a sailor uniform, captain's hat and a long white beard.

Sound Effects: Thunder and rain, optional theme music.

Notes: This is an adaptation of the sketch "The Day After Tomorrow Show," which appears in our first book, *Isaac Air Freight: The Works* (page 59, © 1997 Foolish Guys, Meriwether Publishing Ltd.). In this adaptation, Noah appears on *The Phil Montague Show* rather than *The Tom Snooter Show.*

1   ANNOUNCER: *(From Off-stage)* **And now, live, America's foremost**
2   **audience participation talk show,** *Montague.* **And here's your**
3   **host, Phil Montague.** *(PHIL enters.)*
4   PHIL: **Umm, would you please indicate with your applause which**
5   **of the following statements you agree with most? First, I**
6   **believe that our world is going great and will survive forever.**
7   *(Pause.)* **OK, how about, I believe that our world is growing in**
8   **decadence and is headed for destruction.** *(Pause.)* **Our guest**
9   **today has been producing a lot of controversy around town.**
10 **He's basically a quiet, simple man, but lately he's been**
11 **receiving a lot of notoriety. Our guest ... Captain or Mr. Noah.**
12 *(NOAH enters carrying an umbrella.)* **Noah would have you**
13 **know that he is extremely concerned about today's morality**
14 **and believes that judgment will soon be upon us. Noah,**
15 **welcome to the show.** *(PHIL and NOAH sit.)*
16 NOAH: **Thank you, Phil. It' a pleasure to be here, and even though**
17 **I personally don't watch your show, I'm sure many people do,**
18 **so it's nice to face the nation, as your show does so well.**
19 PHIL: **To begin with, Noah, as you realize, all the people in town**
20 **have been talking about this boat-shaped thing you're**
21 **building downtown there on the corner of Washington and**
22 **Fig. Can you tell us what you're building there? A fancy**
23 **casino? A massage parlor? What?**
24 NOAH: **No, Phil. I'm just building a boat — an ark, if you prefer.**
25 PHIL: **And this ark, as you say — it's quite large, isn't it?**
26 NOAH: **Yes it is, Phil, and I might add it's the finest aquatic vessel**
27 **ever built. Solid gopher wood.**
28 PHIL: **It is a beaut. How long have you been working on it?**
29 NOAH: **Phil, I've been working on it for one hundred and twenty**
30 **years now, and I'm just days away from completion.**
31 PHIL: **Now rumor has it that you're putting animals on it. What's**
32 **the scoop?**
33 NOAH: **Yes, Phil, I'm loading the ark with a male and female of**
34 **every species of bird, reptile and animal.**
35 PHIL: **I see. It must be kind of hard to tell in some cases, though ...**

1   birds, snakes, that sort of thing.
2   NOAH: Well, as the Lord leads.
3   PHIL: Ah, now, this gets to the real question, a question that cuts
4   right to the bone. Why are you doing all of this?
5   NOAH: Well, Phil, if I may be serious for just a moment.
6   PHIL: I wish you would.
7   NOAH: Today we have so much criminal activity, sexual
8   perversion and just basic unrighteous living. So much of
9   man's lifestyle is an abomination in the sight of God. I mean,
10   this is not the kind of world that God intended for creation.
11   Well, God has been patient, but now he's going to bring his
12   wrath upon all of humankind for their evil rebellion and
13   turning from his divine plan.
14 PHIL: Now hold on a second. That's quite a mouthful. How's he
15   supposed to do this, anyway?
16 NOAH: Well, Phil, he's going to flood the entire earth by making it
17   rain for forty days and forty nights.
18 PHIL: Wait a minute. I think we're playing the fool's game here,
19   and I'm the fool.
20 NOAH: Yes, you are, Phil. You see, only my family and I will be
21   saved.
22 PHIL: Well, that's not fair! If what you're saying is true, and this
23   God of yours is really angry, why didn't he tell someone? He
24   could have taken an ad out in the paper or come on the show.
25   I would've gladly had him on the show.
26 NOAH: Phil, God has been warning mankind for some time now.
27   But no one's listening. People have been so busy taking care of
28   themselves that they haven't slowed down long enough to seek
29   God or his plan for us.
30 PHIL: Now how do you know all of this?
31 NOAH: Well, God speaks to me.
32 PHIL: What … ya got one of those cell phones there on the boat or
33   something?
34 NOAH: No, God just talks to me.
35 PHIL: Come on, I've been around gods all of my life. I've got three

1   idols in the kitchen alone, and I've never heard a peep out of

2   'em.

3   NOAH: That's because they're just hunks of wood. I'm talking

4   about the living God.

5   PHIL: I'll tell ya what you're talking about. You're talking about

6   bringing people down. You know, there's a lot of people out

7   there trying to do their best. And the world is hard out there.

8   Then a guy like you comes around and says, "You're not doing

9   this, you're not doing that" … judging everyone. Let me tell

10   ya, people aren't going to stand for it. The kids even have an

11   expression for it … "Choke me with a fork."

12   NOAH: No, Phil, that's "Gag me with a spoon" … and no one's said

13   that for years.

14   PHIL: Whatever. We're about out of time. Is the caller there?

15   CALLER: *(From Off-stage)* Yes. Noah, there must be a good side to

16   the story. Is there any hope for mankind? I mean, how do guys

17   like Phil and me get on this boat of yours?

18   NOAH: That's a good question. Yes, there is a good side to the

19   story. If you will humble yourself, call upon the Lord and turn

20   from your sinful ways, then God will forgive you and you will

21   be saved.

22   PHIL: And if we don't, we're pretty much in the same boat? Or out

23   of it, as the case may be?

24   NOAH: I don't know, you may not have to worry, Phil.

25   PHIL: How's that?

26   NOAH: You're so full of hot air, you just might float.

27   PHIL: Yeah, well, we'll see. Ah, ladies and gentlemen, we only have

28   a few moments left. I'd like to thank my guest for this evening.

29   Noah, good luck with this ark you're building and this God of

30   yours. I suppose he's important to you too. But I really want

31   to encourage you to look into making that ark into a massage

32   parlor or casino. You could do the community a service and

33   make yourself a profit.

34   NOAH: I already am a prophet.

35   PHIL: Well, let's not get into that again. That's all water under the

1   **bridge. And thank you, ladies and gentlemen, for your**
2   **questions and opinions.**
3   ANNOUNCER: *(Off-stage)* **You've been watching *The Phil Montague***
4   ***Show*, brought to you by Miss Clearhold hair spray — hair**
5   **spray of the stars. Marlo uses it, and so does Phil.** *(Optional*
6   *theme music plays. Thunder and rain sounds. NOAH puts up*
7   *umbrella, gives a thumbs-up towards heaven, and exits. A*
8   *panicked PHIL follows.)*
9
10
11
12
13
14
15
16
17
18
19
20
21
22
23
24
25
26
27
28
29
30
31
32
33
34
35

Motel Williams

By Dan Rupple

Cast: Announcer, Son, Daughter, Wife, Husband, Motel Williams.

Setting: A motel. Place a double bed and two twin beds at Center Stage. Since that's not very practical, you can improvise with tables covered with blankets and pillows.

Props: Microphone.

Costumes: Pajamas for Son, Daughter and Husband. Street clothes for Wife. Suit and tie for Motel Williams.

1 *(SON and DAUGHTER are sleeping. WIFE is in street clothes in*
2 *bed with HUSBAND, who is in pajamas but wide awake, enjoying*
3 *the goings-on.)*
4 ANNOUNCER: *(From Off-stage)* You're on vacation with your
5 family. You've been driving so long, the broken clock on the
6 dash has been right three times. It's time to stop. The kids
7 want Best Western, Ramada or America's Innkeeper. But not
8 you. You stay where inquiring minds stay, where conversation
9 is king. You stay at Motel Williams. *(MOTEL enters.)*
10 MOTEL: *(Speaks into microphone.)* Today on Motel Williams,
11 family vacations. Do they draw families together or tear them
12 apart? *(To SON)* What are your thoughts on this?
13 SON: I'm trying to sleep.
14 MOTEL: Is this a way of avoiding confrontation, or do you fear the
15 truth?
16 WIFE: *(To HUSBAND)* The Holiday Inn had a vacancy.
17 HUSBAND: Are you kidding? This guy's great!
18 MOTEL: *(To DAUGHTER)* What if everyone was on vacation?
19 What if everyone just got up, quit school, quit work and went
20 to Disney World? Where would we be?
21 DAUGHTER: Get that microphone out of my face.
22 MOTEL: She brings up a good point. Has lack of recreation left
23 our workaholic nation bitter and irritable?
24 HUSBAND: *(To WIFE)* Is he great or what?
25 WIFE: Honey, I want to get ready for bed.
26 HUSBAND: Go ahead.
27 WIFE: I'm not changing with a strange man in the room.
28 HUSBAND: He's no stranger. He's seen it all.
29 ANNOUNCER: *(From Off-stage)* That's right. This is Motel
30 Williams. You've had a day of stupid driving songs, license
31 plate games and "Roll down the window; Dad had chili." It's
32 time for professional conversation — the conversation at
33 Motel Williams.
34 MOTEL: *(To WIFE)* What kind of man puts his family in a car and
35 transports them across the nation? Is this a man who's happy

1   at home?
2   HUSBAND: Wow, fascinating.
3   DAUGHTER: I'm sleeping in the car. *(Exits.)*
4   SON: Good job, Dad. I'll never forget your immortal words, "The
5   Hilton's on the wrong side of the road." That's why they have
6   overpasses!
7   ANNOUNCER: *(From Off-stage)* No more sitting in your hotel
8   room *watching* TV — you'll be *on* TV. Stop by. Motel
9   Williams ... the lights, camera and action are always on.
10   MOTEL: So what about these mints they leave on your pillow? Do
11   you think it's healthy to eat candy right before you go to bed?
12   WIFE: I just want to go to bed!
13   MOTEL: When we return, we'll be joined by maids who go
14   through your luggage. Be right back. *(MOTEL exits.)*
15   HUSBAND: I knew that was true.
16   WIFE: I'm gonna use his head for a makeup mirror.
17
18
19
20
21
22
23
24
25
26
27
28
29
30
31
32
33
34
35

My Mouth Speaketh

By Dan Rupple

Cast: Announcer, Rev. Moe Tormouth, Teenage Boy, optional extras.

Setting: A television set with three areas: the pulpit at Center Stage, the dinner table at one side (with assorted dishes on top) and the baptismal at the other side.

Props: None.

Costumes: A suit and tie for Rev. Moe Tormouth and a baptismal robe for Teenage Boy.

Notes: Extras may sleep and snore while Rev. Moe Tormouth is preaching and also sit around the dinner table.

1   *(REV. MOE TORMOUTH is at the pulpit, pantomiming preaching*
2   *with wide gestures as Off-stage ANNOUNCER speaks.)*
3   ANNOUNCER: *(From Off-stage)* **Coming soon on this network,** *My*
4   *Mouth Speaketh,* **with Rev. Moe Tormouth — the wordy and**
5   **sometimes realistic story of a Midwestern pastor in a**
6   **shrinking farm community. Hang on to your ears, or he'll talk**
7   **them off.**
8   REV. MOE TORMOUTH: *(Now audible)* **And I believe that this is**
9   **another example of what I've been talking about this**
10   **morning. And now, precious brethren, as we move into the**
11   **final two hours of today's message, I think it is time to realize**
12   **the reality in the age-old proverb, which I personally reflect**
13   **on from time to time, usually after I have a nice hot bath, a**
14   **glass of milk, and I'm curled up on my favorite chair ... did I**
15   **tell you I got it reupholstered? Yeah, a nice vinyl, but that "A**
16   **man isn't judged by how much he loves, but rather by how**
17   **much he is love." Yes, the truth of this statement rings out to**
18   **us, even though it's not in the Bible. It's probably not even**
19   **scriptural, but it is from** *The Wizard of Oz,* **which was one**
20   **great movie. Which reminds me of a story. When I was young,**
21   **oh, about eight or nine, I went to the theater. Back then it**
22   **cost ...** *(Resumes preaching pantomime as ANNOUNCER speaks,*
23   *moving from the pulpit to the dinner table, where he bows his head*
24   *after he sits.)*
25   ANNOUNCER: *(From Off-stage)* **Yes,** *My Mouth Speaketh* **with**
26   **Rev. Moe Tormouth, in a show that brings tears, depression**
27   **and lethargy to all, no matter how strong or immune you are.**
28   **This slow-moving serial will make you glad you aren't there to**
29   **hear** *My Mouth Speaketh.*
30   REV. MOE TORMOUTH: *(Audibly)* **And Lord, as we are joined**
31   **together to thank you for this food, we recall the way you**
32   **provide so abundantly for us. And of course, these potatoes**
33   **remind us of how we are so similar to them. Oh, not exactly,**
34   **but there are important parallels. We both have eyes and skin,**
35   **but the important part is what's inside, and I don't mean**

1   **butter or sour cream and chives, but the true meat of the**
2   **matter. And as people, we are so diverse — some mashed,**
3   **some escalloped, some hash browns ...** *(Resumes preaching*
4   *pantomime as he crosses to the baptismal. Skinny TEENAGE*
5   *BOY enters and stands in the baptismal, shivering.)*
6   **ANNOUNCER:** *(From Off-stage)* **Rev. Moe Tormouth, a man who**
7   **never hears from God because he never stops talking. A man**
8   **with a simple message that he daily makes more complicated.**
9   **REV. MOE TORMOUTH:** *(Audibly)* **And now as we baptize this**
10   **young man, we are thankful for the opportunity to follow you**
11   **in obedience. As your word says, "Be ye baptized," and we**
12   **thank you for all of these people — friends, relatives and**
13   **fellow brethren — for being present here with us. And now I**
14   **baptize you in the name of the Father, Son and Holy Ghost.**
15   *(Dunks TEENAGE BOY and holds under.)* **Oh, that reminds me,**
16   **before I forget, I've been receiving a lot of criticism lately**
17   **from various people in this congregation. They have been**
18   **wondering why I never quote or teach from the Bible, but**
19   **rather use my personal experiences and opinions. Well, I**
20   **believe, why talk about old biblical stories when God**
21   **continues to give me fresh and exciting occurrences that**
22   **happen personally in my life? Now these things might not**
23   **relate to you directly, they might not even be of any**
24   **importance to you, but hey, I got to talk about something.**
25   *(Resumes preaching pantomime, continuing to hold TEENAGE*
26   *BOY under.)*
27   **ANNOUNCER:** *(From Off-stage)* ***My Mouth Speaketh*** **— so real it's**
28   **boring. One man of the cloth with the gift of gab. Rev. Moe**
29   **Tormouth in** ***My Mouth Speaketh*,** **coming soon on this**
30   **network. You'll have plenty of time to see it — it runs on**
31   **forever.** *(TEENAGE BOY fights to come up, gasping and*
32   *choking.)*
33
34
35

Rescue 777

By Dan Rupple

Cast: William Shaftner, Jerry 1 (for the studio), Jerry 2 (for the reenactments), Monica, Daniel, Elderly Couple (nonspeaking roles).

Setting: A street in front of a high school, late at night. Stage Right is the school area. If an old school locker is available, place it there. Stage Left is the dispatch area. Set up a small table or desk and chair.

Props: Business card, two cell phones, telephone headset.

Costumes: Trench coat for William Shaftner and casual clothes for the others. Jerry needs a coat.

1   *(MONICA, a fortyish, plain-Jane dispatcher, sits at her dispatch*
2   *desk at Stage Left. WILLIAM SHAFTNER stands at Center*
3   *Stage.)*
4   **WILLIAM SHAFTNER:** *(Overly dramatic)* **Uptown High School.**
5   **It's quiet now, but come daylight, this campus will be**
6   **transformed by the sounds of laughter, lockers, learning ...**
7   **and the unheard sounds of loneliness. Lost in the chaotic noise**
8   **is a desperate cry for help. Help that you'll hear about tonight**
9   **on ... *Rescue 777*.** *(WILLIAM SHAFTNER exits. JERRY 1 enters*
10   *school area Stage Right.)*
11   **JERRY 1: It was about 8:15. I went by the high school to get a book**
12   **from my locker. I really didn't care about my homework; it**
13   **was just a good reason to get out of the house. My parents**
14   **were on me like a bad haircut on Sinead O'Connor.** *(JERRY 1*
15   *exits. JERRY 2 enters from Stage Left and walks across the stage,*
16   *as if walking down the school hallway to his locker. He reenacts*
17   *the narrative. JERRY 1 continues speaking, but from Off-stage.)*
18   **When I got to my locker, for some reason it wouldn't open.**
19   *(JERRY 2 pantomimes trying to open his locker.)* **I couldn't help**
20   **thinking how much of this was like my life. I'd tried every**
21   **combination: drugs, partying, running away, becoming a**
22   **Trekkie — nothing worked. I couldn't unlock myself. I was**
23   **really feeling desperate. I was in a panic. I thought, shine the**
24   **locker, shine the book, shine my whole life.** *(JERRY 2 paces*
25   *nervously. JERRY 1 enters Stage Right. When JERRY 1 talks,*
26   *JERRY 2 freezes.)* **Wait a minute. I wasn't really talking**
27   **suicide. I mean, I just saw my picture for the yearbook. Total**
28   **geek. No way was I gonna leave that as a legacy. OK, you can**
29   **go to the reenactment now.** *(JERRY 1 exits and JERRY 2*
30   *unfreezes. JERRY 1 continues speaking from Off-stage.)* **Then I**
31   **find this little card in my coat pocket** *(JERRY 2 takes business*
32   *card out of his pocket)***, and I say, "Hey, I remember when I got**
33   **it."** *(DANIEL, a not-too-hip, not-too-nerdy 17-year-old enters*
34   *and pantomimes conversing with JERRY 2.)* **There's this**
35   **Christian dude on campus, Daniel. We call him the Divine**

1   Dweeb. He's actually a pretty nice guy, but we mode him
2   anyway ... you know, knock his books, dump his lunch. But
3   one day he was talking with me, and he gave me this card —
4   "Rescue 777." *(DANIEL exits.)* I'm not sure why, but I called
5   it. *(JERRY 2 takes out his cell phone and pantomimes talking.)*
6   MONICA: When Jerry called, I knew he was desperate. The time
7   was right. I had to act fast. There was already a unit in his
8   area. *(An ELDERLY COUPLE walks across the stage and exits on*
9   *the other side.)* But they weren't right for the job. I needed
10   someone who could relate to Jerry. Someone God had already
11   placed in his life. *(DANIEL enters Stage Left and talks on his cell*
12   *phone.)*
13   DANIEL: When the dispatcher called, I was late. I was trying to
14   get to my youth group. I'm thinking, "Bummer, they never
15   call when it's convenient." But when they told me the deal, I
16   couldn't believe it! Jerry Glummacher! I mean, this guy's the
17   scourge of the school. *(Beat)* But hey, I took the call.
18   *(Pantomimes talking. WILLIAM SHAFTNER enters.)*
19   WILLIAM SHAFTNER: Daniel raced to the school. *(DANIEL runs*
20   *to school area.)* He wasn't sure what he would encounter.
21   Maybe it was an ambush. Maybe he'd find his pants on the
22   top of the flagpole. Maybe he'd spend the rest of the night with
23   his head stuck in the trash can. He said a quick prayer.
24   *(DANIEL bows his head, then joins JERRY 2.)* When Daniel
25   arrived, he found Jerry, a radically hurting victim. He had to
26   act fast. No time for a lengthy theological debate — just the
27   basics, the Gospel truth. *(WILLIAM SHAFTNER exits.)*
28   DANIEL: As we started talking, it was obvious that God had
29   gone before me. Jerry was broken — no more pride, no more
30   anger ... no more shoving my head in my macaroni and
31   cheese at lunch. Jerry's lifelong struggles had exhausted him.
32   He was more than ready to start again, God's way. *(JERRY 1*
33   *enters as DANIEL and JERRY 2 bow their heads.)*
34   JERRY 1: When Daniel prayed with me, I suddenly saw
35   everything differently, like someone opened my eyes. I thought

1   of all the times I ragged on him. I just thank God that he
2   never gave up on me. *(JERRY 1 exits.)*
3 **DANIEL:** It really makes you feel good to be able to help someone
4   like that. You share with someone for so long, and sometimes
5   you get ragged on, then you wait for it to sink in. But in God's
6   timing, you reap. It's this kind of call that makes being part of
7   *Rescue 777* so exciting. And the reward is being part of the
8   harvest. *(WILLIAM SHAFTNER enters.)*
9 **WILLIAM SHAFTNER:** A desperate call in the night, someone
10   running to the rescue and a saved life. All because someone
11   was there, trained in the truth. A caring soul who made his
12   friends aware of *Rescue 777. (Looks back at school area.)* High
13   school evangelism. Hmmm, the final frontier. The final
14   frontier? Wait a minute. *(As he walks away)* Why does that
15   sound so familiar? It does have a ring to it ... the final
16   frontier?

Searchlight — Sincere Love

By Dan Rupple

Cast: Anchor 1, Anchor 2, Bob, Jan, Wayne, Darlene.

Setting: The *Searchlight* television set, and live action from Bob and Jan's living room. *Searchlight* should be at Stage Left, with a desk and chairs for the anchors and a sign with the name of the show. Bob and Jan's living room should be at Stage Right and may be as simple as four chairs arranged in an inverted V. Other living room extras may be added as desired (plants, a lamp, a small table, etc.).

Props: A scrapbook and four plates and four forks ("dessert") on a tray.

Costumes: Suits (and ties, if men) for the anchors and casual attire for the couples.

1   (*ANCHOR 1 and ANCHOR 2 are seated behind a desk. JAN,*
2   *BOB, WAYNE and DARLENE sit in the living room and freeze.*)
3   **ANCHOR 1: Hello, and welcome once again to *Searchlight*. I'm**
4   **your *Searchlight* anchor, _____, *(Insert real name)***
5   **along with _____ *(Insert real name of ANCHOR 2.)*. One**
6   **thing we all seek in our communities and in the world in**
7   **general is peace and harmony with one another. But as much**
8   **as we desire this, it often eludes us. At *Searchlight*, we believe**
9   **that to find love, we must go to the author of love, our Creator,**
10   **and follow his principles for healthy relationships.**
11   **ANCHOR 2: _____, *(Insert name of ANCHOR 1)* tonight we**
12   **take a look at the principle of sincerity in loving others. Let's**
13   **join our hidden *Searchlight* camera as we focus in on what**
14   **appears to be a violation of this principle.** *(The action shifts to*
15   *the living room of BOB and JAN's house. WAYNE and DARLENE*
16   *are their guests.*)
17   **JAN:** *(All unfreeze.)* **Bob and I are so glad that you two could come**
18   **for dinner tonight.**
19   **BOB: Jan and I have really been looking forward to it. I know how**
20   **busy you are.**
21   **WAYNE:** *(Facetiously)* **Are you kidding? We're *never* too busy to**
22   **be with *you* guys.**
23   **DARLENE:** *(Even more facetiously)* **Yeah, on Wayne's and my list**
24   **of people we like to spend time with, you're in the top six or**
25   **seven hundred.**
26   **JAN:** *(Unaware she's just been put down)* **Darlene, that makes us feel**
27   **so good because we really love you two.**
28   **DARLENE: Oh, there's so much to say about what we think of you**
29   **and Bob.**
30   **WAYNE: Yeah, an evening with you is like listening to golf on the**
31   **radio. So much excitement.**
32   **BOB: You know, we should get together more often.**
33   **WAYNE: Oh, Bob, understatement city. Tomorrow I'm going to**
34   **check my calendar and clear any free time I have to spend**
35   **with you. Maybe I can take a few months off.**

1   JAN: Oh, wouldn't that be fun?

2   **WAYNE and DARLENE:** *(Together)* **Really!**

3   BOB: Jan's got to cook you her famous tuna rolls.

4   WAYNE: Tuna rolls? I'd rather have tuna rolls than lobster. Isn't

5   that right, Darlene?

6   DARLENE: Sure, but how could you ever top the ham shank

7   casserole you served tonight? It put Denny's to shame.

8   JAN: Thank you, Darlene. I'll call you with the recipe tomorrow.

9   DARLENE: Would you? I won't tie up the phone for a minute.

10   JAN: Great. Now if you'll excuse me for just a second, I'll be right

11   back with dessert. *(Exit JAN.)*

12   BOB: So, Wayne, what do you think of our house?

13   WAYNE: Bob, it's incredible. I haven't seen this kind of interior

14   decorating even in some motels.

15   BOB: Gee, thanks. Darlene, these are the pictures of our vacation.

16   We went to Wyoming. *(BOB hands scrapbook to DARLENE.)*

17   DARLENE: Oh, what a great place to visit. So much barrenness.

18   WAYNE: I'm so glad they're in color — every shade of brown

19   imaginable.

20   BOB: I'm gonna give Jan a hand in the kitchen. You just enjoy the

21   pictures.

22   WAYNE: Maybe we could borrow them for a few weeks.

23   BOB: Feel free.

24   WAYNE: They're so riveting. *(Exit BOB.)* I've never been so bored

25   since that all-day seminar on how to make sun tea.

26   DARLENE: No kidding. Why'd we ever come?

27   WAYNE: Bob's been bugging me for months. What could I say? He

28   *did* loan me his car when ours was in the shop, and the mower,

29   and the … *(Enter BOB and JAN with dessert.)*

30   JAN: Here it is!

31   DARLENE: Jan, this looks like a Sara Lee advertisement.

32   BOB: Jan got the recipe off the back of a cereal box.

33   DARLENE: Most great chefs do.

34   WAYNE: It's delicious. Well, we could stay forever, but we've got

35   to get home.

1 JAN: So soon? You haven't finished your dessert. *(WAYNE and*
2 *DARLENE look at each other, then begin shoving their dessert*
3 *into their mouths to finish it.)*
4 DARLENE: No, we have to go. I left the water on in the bathtub.
5 WAYNE: And our refrigerator door is wide open.
6 BOB: Oh? You'd better go. But Wayne, give me a call to set up
7 when we can get together again.
8 WAYNE: It's a priority. I can tell we're gonna be tight.
9 JAN: And Darlene, I won't forget to call with that ham shank
10 casserole recipe.
11 DARLENE: Thanks, Jan. I'll sleep better tonight.
12 BOB and JAN: *(Together)* Good-bye.
13 WAYNE and DARLENE: Yeah, good night. *(Exit DARLENE and*
14 *WAYNE.)*
15 JAN: Darlene and Wayne are so caring and sincere.
16 BOB: I think we're developing quite a friendship. *(JAN and BOB*
17 *freeze while the action shifts back to the* Searchlight *desk.)*
18 ANCHOR 1: Well, I think the violation of tonight's principle, "Let
19 your love be sincere" (Romans 12:9, author's paraphrase) is
20 obvious.
21 ANCHOR 2: You know, we all are guilty of wrong attitudes from
22 time to time, but *Searchlight* is shining on the blatant
23 individual who gives no regard to godly standards. And you
24 know, _____ *(Insert ANCHOR 1's real name)*, the sad
25 part is missing the benefits that come from following these
26 principles.
27 ANCHOR 1: So take heed because our *Searchlight* is everywhere,
28 and we never know who or what it might find. You can fool
29 some people some of the time, but eventually *Searchlight* will
30 discover you. This is _____ *(ANCHOR 1's real name)*,
31 along with _____ *(ANCHOR 2's real name)*. Good
32 night from *Searchlight*.
33
34
35

Trinity Life Insurance

By Dave Toole

Cast: Arnie Funkwyler, Salesperson, Customer.

Setting: TV studio and Customer's home. Place a podium at Center Stage for Arnie. A door is needed for Customer's house (or you can pantomime one if not available).

Props: None.

Costumes: Suits and ties for Arnie and Salesperson. Customer may be dressed casually.

1   (*Door knock. Door opens.*)
2   SALESPERSON: Good day, sir. Paul Molly for Acme Life
3   Insurance, and I want to ask you about ...
4   CUSTOMER: I won't be needing any life insurance. You see, I
5   won't be dying.
6   SALESPERSON: You what?
7   CUSTOMER: Well, I'm a Christian, and we don't have to worry
8   about all that.
9   SALESPERSON: What about your wife and children? You know
10   we ...
11   CUSTOMER: Sorry, they're saved too.
12   SALESPERSON: You say Christians don't have to worry about
13   death? Tell me more.
14   CUSTOMER: Gladly. You see, Jesus Christ ... (*CUSTOMER and*
15   *SALESPERSON pantomime. The sound of a clock ticking is*
16   *heard.*)
17   ARNIE: Ever notice how time keeps on tickin', tickin', tickin' into
18   the future? How every swing of the pendulum takes you
19   further from yesterday and closer to that date with destiny? If
20   you think we're only born to grow up and die, then I want to
21   talk to you.
22   Hello. I'm Arnie Funkwyler for Trinity Life Insurance. Has
23   it ever occurred to you that most life insurance companies
24   really sell death policies? They promise to pay your relatives
25   when you go as long as you pay them while you're here. But
26   Trinity guarantees its people something *no* one else can offer.
27   Life! Eternal life. And not some dull, dreary existence — we
28   mean life, and that more abundantly!
29   You'll experience love, joy, peace, patience, kindness,
30   goodness, faithfulness, gentleness and even self-control in a
31   way you never understood before. No longer will you have to
32   fear what's around the next corner, be depressed about the
33   last corner, be discouraged by the number of corners or feel
34   guilty about cutting corners when you get your life on the
35   straight and narrow. (*ARNIE exits. CUSTOMER and*

1 *SALESPERSON resume conversation audibly.)*
2 **CUSTOMER: Don't get me wrong. I'm not saying I don't have to**
3 **go, just that when the time comes, I know where I'm going.**
4 **SALESPERSON; Wow, there's no way I can ever top a deal like**
5 **that, but what about fire insurance?**
6 **CUSTOMER: Nope, I got that covered too!** *(Waves to*
7 *SALESPERSON and shuts door. SALESPERSON exits.)*
8
9
10
11
12
13
14
15
16
17
18
19
20
21
22
23
24
25
26
27
28
29
30
31
32
33
34
35

The Truelight Zone

By Dan Rupple

Cast: Rob Sterling, Man 1, Man 2, Marlene.

Setting: An elevator, which may be mimed. The scenario takes place on a television show. A podium is at Stage Right or Left.

Props: None.

Costumes: Suits and ties for Rob Sterling, Man 1 and Man 2. Rob's should be a black suit with a white shirt and a skinny black tie. Marlene should wear casual clothes.

1 *(ROB STERLING is at a podium off to the side. MAN 1 walks out*
2 *and pushes button to get elevator. MAN 2 walks out and pushes*
3 *elevator button also. MAN 1 gives MAN 2 a weird look.)*
4 **ROB STERLING: Two men, anxiously awaiting the arrival of an**
5 **elevator. A simple elevator that takes hundreds of people daily**
6 **on its predictable trek, up and down the shafts of daily living.**
7 **Simple and predictable, yes; but man can never dismiss the**
8 **unexpected, for these unsuspecting bystanders are about to**
9 **embark on a crash course on the ups and downs of human**
10 **emotions. Now we reach into life's hidden expressions on *The***
11 ***Truelight Zone.***
12 **MAN 1: Excuse me, but why did you push that button?**
13 **MAN 2: Ah, to get the elevator.**
14 **MAN 1: That's what I thought. Don't you think that my push was**
15 **sufficient?**
16 **MAN 2: Well, sure. I just didn't know if you had pushed it or not.**
17 **MAN 1: You think that I would stand here, waiting for the elevator,**
18 **and not push the button?**
19 **MAN 2: Well, no I guess I did realize that you had pushed it.**
20 **MAN 1: You did realize?**
21 **MAN 2: Yeah, I guess.**
22 **MAN 1: But you pushed it anyway. *(Pause)* Was there something**
23 **wrong with my push?**
24 **MAN 2: No. I didn't even see your push.**
25 **MAN 1: Then what made you feel as though you had to push it**
26 **yourself? Do I look as though I'm incapable of a good push?**
27 **MAN 2: Look, I'm not going to argue with you. I'm sorry. I**
28 **shouldn't have pushed the button again. I've had a bad day,**
29 **and I made a mistake. So forget it.**
30 **MAN 1: How can I forget this? All of my life, people have**
31 **questioned my value and my ability. Now answer me. Do I**
32 **look as though I'm incapable of a good push?**
33 **MAN 2: No. *(Pause.)* I just wasn't sure if it took.**
34 **MAN 1: Didn't take? For an elevator button push not to take, the**
35 **pusher would have to be a jerk or something. Are you saying**

1   that I'm a jerk?

2   MAN 2: I'm not saying that you're anything. Just leave me alone.

3   MAN 1: Leave you alone. So, not only are my abilities so

4   insignificant that they are utterly unimportant to your

5   existence, but now you insult my very potential for a

6   meaningful relationship. Even a jerk can maintain a valuable

7   friendship.

8   MAN 2: I did not call you a jerk. I don't think that you're

9   incapable of pushing an elevator button or maintaining a

10   relationship. Look, I'm sure that your push took. I must have

11   been out of my mind to push it. I'm sorry the whole thing

12   happened, and I can guarantee that it will never happen

13   again.

14   MAN 1: Typical! But I want you to know that your guilt feelings

15   don't alleviate the damage you've done to my self-image.

16   *(MARLENE walks up.)*

17   MARLENE: OK, Larry. I'm ready to go. Where's the elevator?

18   MAN 1: Are you asking me?

19   MARLENE: No, I'm asking my husband.

20   MAN 1: Good, because there is no way a jerk like me could give

21   you a reasonable answer.

22   MARLENE: Gee, you shouldn't think so low of yourself.

23   MAN 1: Tell your husband that.

24   MARLENE: What?

25   MAN 2: For crying out loud!

26   MAN 1: After I had already pushed the button, he came up and re-

27   pushed it.

28   MARLENE: Boy, Larry, that was pretty rude.

29   MAN 2: Marlene, I didn't realize he had pushed it.

30   MARLENE: To stand here and not push it, this poor man would

31   have to be a jerk or something. *(To MAN 1)* You'll have to

32   excuse him. He hasn't been himself lately.

33   MAN 2: Marlene, what are you talking about?

34   MARLENE: Oh, Larry, you know what I'm talking about.

35   MAN 2: No, I don't. What?

1 MAN 1: Yeah, what?

2 MARLENE: Well, you've just been so closed, so distracted.

3 MAN 2: Distracted?

4 MARLENE: We never talk anymore.

5 MAN 2: We talk.

6 MARLENE: Sure, surface junk, like where's the paper? When's

7   dinner? But he never really opens up to me.

8 MAN 1: That's terrible. I'll bet he never asks you how you are

9   doing, either.

10 MAN 2: Will you stay out of this?

11 MARLENE: My friend can say anything he wants.

12 MAN 2: Your friend? Marlene, he's a total stranger.

13 MARLENE: Are you kidding? This man is sensitive and deep.

14 MAN 2: And you thought I was a jerk.

15 MARLENE: Don't avoid the issue. When was the last time you

16   asked me how I was doing?

17 MAN 2: I don't know. Let's say Tuesday.

18 MARLENE: No, it was May 12, 1979.

19 MAN 1: Boy, you've got a great memory.

20 MARLENE: It was between the commercials of the IBM

21   championship.

22 MAN 2: That's the NBA.

23 MARLENE: IBM, NBA, doesn't matter. It's like I don't even exist.

24   Can you imagine what it's like to sit in a house all day,

25   cleaning and taking care of small children?

26 MAN 1: Sounds like a thankless job.

27 MARLENE: To say the least. All day long I look forward to him

28   coming home. I mean, someone to talk to with a bigger

29   vocabulary than the dog.

30 MAN 1: Which I'm sure he has.

31 MARLENE: And does he show me any attention? No way! The

32   only way he'll look at me is if I steal something and make the

33   five o'clock news.

34 MAN 2: Oh sure, our not talking is all my fault.

35 MARLENE: I suppose it's my fault.

1   MAN 2: Maybe so. Who wants to talk with a nag?

2   MARLENE: A nag?

3   MAN 2: Yes. *(To MAN 1)* Every time I tell her anything, she

4   criticizes. I mean, like I don't have enough pressure. Look,

5   you're a man, you know the score. It's a dog-eat-dog world

6   out there.

7   MAN 1: You're telling me.

8   MAN 2: Right, pal. People are just waiting for you to fall. There's

9   this guy at work, if I make one slight mistake, he goes right to

10   the boss.

11   MAN 1: I bet he wants your job.

12   MAN 2: No kidding he wants my job. But he's not going to get it.

13   I've worked hard for that position.

14   MAN 1: For sure, and who does this leech think he is, trying to take

15   it right out from under your schnoz?

16   MARLENE: I didn't know someone was after your job.

17   MAN 2: Well, someone is, and my house payment's going up fifty

18   dollars next month, the downstairs plumbing's going bad and

19   I think the Buick threw a rod.

20   MAN 1: If you threw a rod, you're talking bucks.

21   MARLENE: Honey, I had no idea.

22   MAN 2: Of course you didn't. You think I'm going to tell you my

23   troubles? *(To MAN 1)* You think I'm going to remind her of

24   what a failure she married? Just give her more ammunition to

25   throw up in my face!

26   MAN 1: You throw up in his face?

27   MARLENE: No, I don't throw up in … that's sickening. Honey, I

28   don't think that you're a failure.

29   MAN 2: Well, then why do you put me down all the time?

30   MARLENE: I don't mean to. Maybe it's just to get your attention.

31   I guess I get mad at you because you don't seem to notice me.

32   MAN 2: Yeah, and I don't talk with you because you're always mad

33   at me.

34   MAN 1: Sounds like a Catch-22.

35   MAN 2: Yeah, I guess it … hey, who are you, anyway?

1   MAN 1: Well, I'm just ...
2   MARLENE: Yeah, and what are you doing sticking your nose in
3   other people's business?
4   MAN 1: I'm just waiting for the elevator.
5   MAN 2: Well, fine, then get the elevator and move on. *(Pushes*
6   *button.)*
7   MAN 1: Excuse me. Why did you push that button?
8   ROB STERLING: A simple setting. An elevator button, a neutral
9   party and a frustrated couple. A couple pent up with
10   suppressed emotions. Feelings and hurts that were left unsaid.
11   Bitterness that might have one day exploded, had they not met
12   up with *The Truelight Zone.*
13
14
15
16
17
18
19
20
21
22
23
24
25
26
27
28
29
30
31
32
33
34
35

Two Guys Camping

By Dan Rupple

Cast: Bert, Ernie.

Setting: A campsite.

Props: Two blankets.

Costumes: Camping attire.

1	(BERT and ERNIE walk in and squat around an imaginary
2	campfire. They have blankets wrapped around themselves.)
3	ERNIE: Ah, this is great. There's nothing like the great outdoors.
4	BERT: I'll say.
5	ERNIE: Two men, out in God's creation, far from the noise of the
6	city, no one else for miles.
7	BERT: Boy, I sure appreciate you inviting me.
8	ERNIE: Of course. You know, when Ben and Jerry and Phil and
9	Don and — well, all the guys — suddenly couldn't make it, I
10	thought, hey, I had the time off from work and I had seen you
11	around church, so why not go for it?
12	BERT: That's right, and there's no better place to get to know one
13	another than camping.
14	ERNIE: You've camped a lot?
15	BERT: Oh, yeah.
16	ERNIE: Umm, as a kid, your dad took you out?
17	BERT: Oh no, this was as an adult. I camped beside freeways,
18	alleyways, cardboard boxes, whatever it took.
19	ERNIE: You were homeless?
20	BERT: 'Fraid so.
21	ERNIE: Boy, that's horrible. Is this a tough world or what?
22	BERT: Yeah, my landlord threw me out, and just because I
23	smashed his head with a rake.
24	ERNIE: *(Startled)* A rake? You smashed his head with a rake?
25	BERT: But I think it was the baseball bat to the ribs that really
26	ticked him off. So out I go, on the streets for six months.
27	ERNIE: *(Looking worried)* A baseball bat! *(Moves away slightly.)*
28	BERT: But hey, I'm a Christian now. That's behind me — under
29	the blood.
30	ERNIE: *(Regaining composure)* Yeah … under the blood. Absolutely.
31	BERT: Praise the Lord.
32	ERNIE: Boy, when I think of the things I did before I was a
33	Christian … One time we threw lemons at cars, then we'd
34	hide behind the bushes. They never knew what hit 'em. Wow,
35	is that crazy or what?

1 BERT: Crazy.
2 ERNIE: But when you're young, sometimes you do stupid things.
3 BERT: Stupid. I heard that. Like the time I was smuggling drugs
4   over the border and I let the DEA officer see my gun.
5 ERNIE: *(Outraged)* **What?!**
6 BERT: Stupid, huh?
7 ERNIE: Smuggling drugs? You were smuggling drugs?
8 BERT: Got three years.
9 ERNIE: Of course you did. You had a gun!
10 BERT: Hey, I only used it twice.
11 ERNIE: *(Shocked)* You used it? You used a gun? I'm here in the
12   middle of nowhere with a homeless, gun-toting drug smuggler?
13 BERT: Yep, but I'm a Christian now. That's all behind me. Under
14   the blood. *(ERNIE hesitates, a little cautious.)*
15 ERNIE: Yeah … that's right … OK, I mean your life gets off track,
16   you go to prison for three years, then God totally changes …
17 BERT: Six years.
18 ERNIE: What?
19 BERT: Six years. I was in for six years.
20 ERNIE: Six years? You just said you were in prison for three years.
21 BERT: No, I said I *got* three years. But they added three more for
22   beating up a guard and leading a prison revolt.
23 ERNIE: You beat up a prison guard?
24 BERT: He tried to short me a blanket. When you're cold, you get
25   desperate. *(ERNIE's really worried now. He looks around.)*
26 ERNIE: Hmm, great fire, huh? Warm fire. That's one warm fire.
27   Do we need another log? How about it? One more log?
28 BERT: *(Doesn't acknowledge what ERNIE's just said.)* But hey, I'm a
29   Christian now. That's as far as the east is from the west (Psalm
30   103:12). I'm a changed man.
31 ERNIE: A changed man, of course … of course, a changed, a saved,
32   a regenerated, sanctified man.
33 BERT: That's me.
34 ERNIE: Sure. We all have skeletons in the closet. Things we've
35   done. I mean, I papered my science teacher's house. I'm not

1	proud of it, but hey … stuff happens. *(Pause)* Boy, six years.
2	What did your family think?
3	BERT: Well, four of my wives didn't care, but the other six were
4	devastated.
5	ERNIE: *(Outraged)* Ten?! You … you had ten wives? This is
6	unbelievable! How does a guy have ten wives? What's wrong
7	with you? How do you live with yourself?
8	BERT: A lot easier than living with ten wives, let me tell you. But
9	why dwell in the past? Hey …
10	BERT AND ERNIE: *(Together)* I'm a Christian now …
11	BERT: That's behind me, forgiven, reconciled, I'm moving on.
12	ERNIE: Ten wives … ten wives. Jail, drugs, guns. It's amazing
13	you're still alive.
14	BERT: Amazing grace, how sweet the sound.
15	ERNIE: *(Resumes fears.)* But you're OK now, right? Things are
16	changed now, right? You're different, right?
17	BERT: Totally. A new creature in Christ.
18	ERNIE: *(Still a little suspicious)* Of course. Well, that's good to hear.
19	*(Long silence)* Boy, it's quiet out here.
20	BERT: Reminds me of waiting in that liquor store for the owner to
21	leave …
22	ERNIE: Oh, no.
23	BERT: Except he didn't leave, and he caught me red-handed with
24	my fingers in the register.
25	ERNIE: *(Stands.)* That was you! I read about that!
26	BERT: Yeah, it was all over the news. But I'm a Christian now …
27	ERNIE: No, I just read about it last week. That just happened!
28	BERT: Don't worry, I tithed the profits.
29	ERNIE: No, you can't do that. What about "Go and sin no more"
30	(John 8:11)?
31	BERT: It says where sin abounds, grace much more abounds
32	(Romans 5:20, author's paraphrase). Hey, I've got grace
33	abounding out my ears.
34	ERNIE: This is crazy. You can't deliberately keep ripping people
35	off and say you're a Christian.

1   BERT: OK, I get it. You're jealous.

2   ERNIE: What?

3   BERT: You're jealous.

4   ERNIE: Jealous? I'm not jealous! *(BERT smiles smugly.)* Jealous of

5   what? A homeless, gun-toting, drug-smuggling, thieving,

6   guard-beating bigamist? What on God's earth would you

7   have that I could possibly be jealous of?

8   BERT: My testimony. You've got to admit, I've got a great

9   testimony.

10   ERNIE: Yeah, and it's growing daily!

11   BERT: Face it — you'd kill to have a testimony like mine.

12   ERNIE: And you obviously have.

13   BERT: Throwing lemons and papering houses doesn't get the

14   word out. But I've been on Christian TV, and I'm ripe for

15   Sally Jesse.

16   ERNIE: The Bible says whoever steals, whoever lies, whoever

17   kills — and you certainly fit all of these categories — should

18   stop doing it.

19   BERT: Look, I don't think we should be nit-picking over

20   theological interpretations.

21   ERNIE: Ugh! *(ERNIE gives up.)* Forget it. Just forget it. *(ERNIE*

22   *rolls over to go to sleep. There is a long silence.)*

23   BERT: Are you asleep?

24   ERNIE: Trying to.

25   BERT: Did you ever wonder why all those other guys decided not

26   to come camping when they heard I was coming? *(ERNIE pops*

27   *up quickly, looking at BERT.)*

28   ERNIE: You know, I think I left the truck open. I'm going to the

29   truck. I'll be right back. *(ERNIE quickly exits.)*

30   BERT: Do you keep your wallet in your pants or your coat? ... Hey,

31   come on, I'm kidding. Don't worry, I'm a Christian now.

32   That's all behind me. *(Follows after him.)*

33

34

35

Way to Go, Ralph

By Dan Rupple

Cast: Ralph's Coworker.

Setting: A promotion party at the office.

Props: None.

Costumes: A suit and tie.

1 (*RALPH'S COWORKER stands at Center Stage, addressing the*
2 *audience as if they are at the promotion party.*)
3 **RALPH'S COWORKER: Well, we're all here to congratulate**
4 **Ralph Mercel on his promotion from our department to a vice**
5 **presidency upstairs.** Now I know a lot of you suspect
6 **animosity, or at least jealousy, between Ralph and me, and**
7 **that's understandable, I guess.** When we found out nine
8 **months ago that someone from our department would get this**
9 **promotion, Ralph and I were the leading candidates.** But let
10 **me say that the man to whom it was the most important got it,**
11 **and congratulations — way to go, Ralph.**
12 **I've known Ralph for nine years, and he is a man of great**
13 **commitment to his job, with unrelenting work habits. I**
14 **remember nights I'd leave here to go out with my wife or to**
15 **midweek church or my kid's school plays, but not Ralph. He**
16 **never once left here for those trivial things. No, Ralph's nose**
17 **was to the grindstone. Way to go, Ralph.**
18 **Yeah, I guess I should've taken a lesson from Ralph. You**
19 **know in the springtime, once a week, I'd leave a half hour**
20 **early to coach our son's Little League team.** (*Shakes his head.*)
21 **Little League! I'm in position for a promotion, and I get**
22 **involved in Little League? But I did enjoy it. By the way,**
23 **Ralph, Ralphie Junior had a great season. He made the all-**
24 **star team. Yeah, Ralph chose to stay here, and hey, that**
25 **overtime adds up. Ralph's BMW dwarfs my Accord. And**
26 **your boat, "The USS Schmooze," it's an impressive thing to**
27 **have, and if I wanted to keep it nice for my clients, I wouldn't**
28 **let my family on it either. Way to go, Ralph.**
29 **I've learned a lot about priorities from the Ralpher here. I**
30 **always tried to get Sundays off, and what did I get? A day of**
31 **rest, a church life and a day with my family. Huh — what's**
32 **that gonna get me? But what did Ralph get? A vice**
33 **presidency! Way to go, Ralph.**
34 **You know, when I get home today, the kids are gonna run**
35 **up to me and welcome me home, and I'll have to tell them I**

1 didn't get the promotion … and they'll say, "Way to go, Dad."
2 But you, Ralph. You'll go back to your apartment, call your
3 kids over at your ex-wife's and tell them, "Hey, don't call me
4 Dad anymore; call me Mr. Vice President." Way to go, Ralph.
5
6
7
8
9
10
11
12
13
14
15
16
17
18
19
20
21
22
23
24
25
26
27
28
29
30
31
32
33
34
35

Isaac Air Freight Discography

Fun in the Son
(Maranatha!, 1978)

In the Air/On the Air
(Maranatha!, 1979)

Foolish Guys...to Confound the Wise
(Maranatha!, 1980)

Snooze Ya Looze
(Maranatha!, 1981)

My Kingdom Come/Thy Kingdom Come
(Maranatha!, 1982)

The Pick of the Litter
(Maranatha!, 1984)

The Freight's Designer Album
(Maranatha!, 1985)

Over Our Heads
(Frontline Records, 1987)

Dave
Toole

Dan
Rupple

About
the Authors

Isaac Air Freight was the best known and most inventive comedy team in a field they almost single-handedly pioneered: Christian comedy. Their unique style of satirical sketch comedy humorously communicates piercing truths about the human condition through the antics of some of the most colorful and real characters you may ever have the pleasure of meeting.

The original members of Isaac Air Freight, Dan Rupple and Dave Toole, teamed up in 1976 with the hope of building a successful comedy writing and performing career. They were able to do just that, but in a way they never expected. They were gaining considerable word-of-mouth attention around Southern California nightclubs when in 1977, they each made a commitment to Christ. The personal changes they were experiencing quickly became evident in their direction as a group. Material that had its basis in cynicism and escapism steadily gave way to comedy that inspired their audiences and offered them an opportunity to re-examine today's values.

In 1978 they recorded their first album, entitled *Fun in the Son*. It was an immediate best-seller among contemporary Christian audiences. By the time their second album, *In the Air/On the Air*, was released, the group's touring schedule had grown enormously, and with it, the appeal for their insightful comic vision. 1980 brought the release of *Foolish Guys ... to Confound the Wise*, an album aimed at the spiritual center of contemporary life both inside and outside the church; a powerful statement in laughter.

In 1981 Dan and Dave began work on *The Isaac Air Show*, a highly successful daily radio feature. The program was syndicated nationwide on over

120 stations. The most popular selections from the show gave birth to two more albums, *Snooze Ya Looze* and *My Kingdom Come/Thy Kingdom Come.*

Extensive touring and numerous television projects brought the group widespread recognition not only within the gospel industry, but with a national, mainstream audience. Their growing popularity brought two more albums aimed at this audience outside the church walls. *The Freight's Designer Album* (1985) and *Over Our Heads* (1987) revealed their growth as artists and as communicators.

In 1987 Dan and Dave limited their engagements to part-time weekend performances, due to their desires to move into different areas of ministry. In 1991 the hilarious fun of Isaac Air Freight came to an end. From there, Dan went on to co-host a highly popular morning talk radio show in Southern California with childhood friend and Christian musician Bob Bennett. In 1990 Dan left radio to work for CBS Television, where he supervised the productions of *The Price Is Right* and *The Late Show with David Letterman.* After ten years at CBS, Dan returned to full-time ministry. He is presently serving as the Executive Pastor at Florence Avenue Foursquare Church in Southern California.

When the team ended in 1991, Dave found a job in sales and today is a successful sales manager for a printing company in Orange County.

Both men have been happily married for well over twenty years and are actively involved with their families. Dan is the father of three and Dave, the father of four.

For now, the group's live appearances are a wonderful memory of the past; but the eternal truths of their sketches are as relevant and true as the day they were first presented.

Order Form

Meriwether Publishing Ltd.
P.O. Box 7710
Colorado Springs, CO 80933-7710
Telephone: (719) 594-4422
Website: www.meriwetherpublishing.com

Please send me the following books:

_____ **Isaac Air Freight: The Works 2 #BK-B243**   **$16.95**
by Dan Rupple and Dave Toole
More sketches from the premier Christian comedy group

_____ **Isaac Air Freight: The Works #BK-B215**   **$16.95**
by Dan Rupple and Dave Toole
Sketches from the premier Christian comedy group

_____ **Service with a Smile #BK-B225**   **$14.95**
by Daniel Wray
52 humorous sketches for Sunday worship

_____ **The Best of the Jeremiah People**   **$14.95**
#BK-B117
by Jim Custer and Bob Hoose
Humorous skits and sketches by a leading Christian repertory group

_____ **Don't Give Up the Script #BK-B204**   **$12.95**
by Robert A. Allen
Writing original sketches for the church

_____ **Divine Comedies #BK-B190**   **$12.95**
by T. M. Williams
A collection of plays for church drama groups

_____ **Sermons Alive! #BK-B132**   **$14.95**
by Paul Neale Lessard
52 dramatic sketches for worship services

These and other fine Meriwether Publishing books are available at your local bookstore or direct from the publisher. Prices subject to change without notice. Check our website or call for current prices.

Name: _____

Organization name: _____

Address: _____

City: _____ State: _____

Zip: _____ Phone: _____

❑ **Check enclosed**

❑ **Visa / MasterCard / Discover #** _____
                                                   Expiration
Signature: _____   *date:* _____
       (required for credit card orders)

Colorado residents: Please add 3% sales tax.
Shipping: Include $2.75 for the first book and 50¢ for each additional book ordered.

❑ *Please send me a copy of your complete catalog of books and plays.*